# ECONOMIC DEVELOPMENT PARABLES

Wongsurawat looks at the history of Thailand since the mid-nineteenth century and uses events to elucidate basic economic models and concepts. He selects defining moments in Thailand's history to convey key economic ideas worthy of classroom discussion.

Written without excessive jargon, the chapters connect complex historical phenomena with broader, transportable economic concepts. The cases range from the signing of the Bowring Treaty in 1855, opening Siam to the forces of globalization, to the Asian Financial Crisis that wreaked havoc on the economy in 1997. Key economic terms are also explained.

Reconnecting the increasingly distant fields of history and economics, this is an appealing text to researchers with an interest in Thailand's economic history, as well as undergraduates undergoing an introductory economics course or overseas program in Thailand.

**Winai Wongsurawat** is an associate professor at the College of Management, Mahidol University, Thailand.

# Routledge Studies in the Modern World Economy

For more information about this series, please visit: www.routledge.com/
Routledge-Studies-in-the-Modern-World-Economy/book-series/SE0432

# Economic Development Parables

## From Siam to Thailand

**Winai Wongsurawat**

LONDON AND NEW YORK

First published 2023
by Routledge
4 Park Square, Milton Park, Abingdon, Oxon, OX14 4RN

and by Routledge
605 Third Avenue, New York, NY 10158

*Routledge is an imprint of the Taylor & Francis Group, an informa business*

© 2023 Winai Wongsurawat

*British Library Cataloguing-in-Publication Data*
A catalogue record for this book is available from the British Library

ISBN: 9781032491295 (hbk)
ISBN: 9781032491288 (pbk)
ISBN: 9781003392262 (ebk)

DOI: 10.4324/9781003392262

Typeset in Times New Roman
by codeMantra

# Contents

# Tables

# Figures

# Acknowledgments

This book grew out of the courses on the political economy of Thailand that I taught at the School of Management at the Asian Institute of Technology, and at the Faculty of Arts at Chulalongkorn University between 2011 and 2015. I am grateful to my students for patiently and cheerfully exploring and learning these topics together with me.

My father supplied the gentle nudge for me to continue working on the book, especially during the times when I may have mentally abandoned the project. My mother expertly edited the drafts, greatly enhancing the readability of each and every chapter. I am responsible for the remaining errors.

I am thankful to the publishers at Routledge for taking a chance on this project.

Finally, I thank my wife for her loving support and for insisting that I complete this project before the arrival of our first child. My son's kicks gave my wife and I great happiness during the final stages of the manuscript preparation. I hope I might just as gently return the nudge one day when he is old enough to browse through these pages.

# Acknowledgments

# 1 Durianomics

## The Economics of the King of Fruits

> *Relevant period*: late 1700s (Early Bangkok)
> *Economic concepts*: external cost

Durian, sometimes referred to as the King of Fruits, is a delicacy native to Southeast Asia. Known for its thorny exterior, and sweet, yellow, custard-like flesh, the fruit possesses a distinctive aroma highly enticing to some but simply unbearable to others. Opinions of the fruit are diametrical – some consider the taste heavenly, while others deem it revolting.

Legend has it that both King Chulalongkorn and his son, Vajiravudh, so despised the smell of durian that the fruit was banned from the palace premises. The *durianophiles* among the day-staff could only enjoy the delicacy when they were not on shift. One young page who came into the King's presence with durian on his breath lived to regret it.

A number of residents of the inner palace did not get to go outside on a regular basis. During durian season, they needed somebody to smuggle the smelly fruit into the palace for them. Creative durian-smuggling techniques included paring away the thorny surface of the fruit to pass it off at the palace entrance as a pomelo. Palace ladies who habitually used padding made of cloth to add volume to their hairdo would sometimes return to the palace wearing a section of durian instead of their hair cushion. Such strategies, though, required that the smuggled fruit be semi-ripe in order to avoid the conspicuous perfume of the perfectly aged fruit.

While durian is well-known across Southeast Asia, Thai durian is considered by many to be the best in the world. Thailand is consistently the top durian exporter. What lies behind Thailand's success? An important factor determining the quality of orchard fruit, such as durian, is breed selection. Durian flowers are known to be pollinated by a variety of species such as bats, spiderhunters, and bees. But why might the breed selection of durian in Thailand hold an advantage over those in other countries?

DOI: 10.4324/9781003392262-1

An orchard tax enacted in early nineteenth-century Siam may have contributed to the country's superior durian breed selection. At the beginning of a new reign, the king would send out commissioners to conduct a census of commercial agriculture in the Bangkok vicinity. The tax on paddy would be estimated by the size of the paddy fields – for example 0.25 baht per rai.[1] Taxes would also be levied on the thriving fruit orchards surrounding the capital. For high-value fruits such as durian, tax would be collected according to the number of mature trees in the orchard. The tax rate on durian was set at an eye-watering rate of *1 baht per tree*.

Surveying agricultural activity in the vicinity of Bangkok at the beginning of a new reign was a task not taken lightly. The missions were rife with opportunities for bribery and extortion. The owner of an orchard, for example, could cut a deal with the commissioner to under-report the number of mature trees on his property. The tax savings would justify a handsome payment to the complicit commissioner. With such deals taking place, the Treasury could be deprived of significant revenue. Attempting to snuff out this felonious behavior, a tradition was conceived to have all commissioners swear before the Emerald Buddha, Siam's most sacred icon, to conduct their surveys with utmost honesty. Arriving at the orchard, the commissioner would be made to swear once more, this time before the site's guardian spirit, just to make sure he had not forgotten his prior oath made in the city.

Let us ponder how such a tax would affect the incentives of an orchard owner. Suddenly, owning a durian tree had become more expensive. In addition to the regular maintenance costs (watering, pruning, etc.), the owner was now liable for sending the Treasury 1 baht for each mature tree standing on his property. How would you expect the owner's behavior to change after the tax came into effect? In an extreme case, the owner could completely avoid the tax by chopping down *all* his durian trees, but such a drastic response would tend to be suboptimal. His best trees – the ones with superb yield both in quantity and quality – would likely still be profitable to keep, *even* with such a tax being levied. Poorer quality trees would be candidates for elimination. The worst would need to go immediately. Such behavior is essentially an accelerated breed selection process induced by an orchard tax!

According to Kukrit Pramote, Thailand's prominent twentieth-century scholar and former prime minister, it is no coincidence that Thailand's most famous durian breeds are local to the areas known to have been subjected to the orchard tax, in particular, the modern-day city of Nonthaburi.

The story of the durian tax as an incentive yields an important economic lesson. For one thing, keeping a tree that produces poor-quality fruit may, through cross-pollination, impose an *external cost* on other orchardists. A low-quality durian tree in one orchard could harm the quality of the next generation of durian trees in neighboring orchards. After all, bats, spiderhunters, and bees do not respect orchard boundaries when going about their business. Chopping down trees that produce sub-standard durian is therefore doing one's neighbors a courtesy and a favor. Taxing economic activities that also inflict external costs on third parties, as we shall see, is a key policy insight that is still immensely relevant in the modern world.

Economics has useful insights about designing incentives to encourage people to make pro-social decisions. When an orchard owner decides whether to keep a tree, he fully takes into consideration his own costs (watering, pruning, lost opportunity to grow something else, etc.) and benefits (the produce, the shade, aesthetics, etc.). Unless anyone complains, however, he is unlikely to worry much about how his neighbors will feel about what he does with his own property. Although his choices may generate extra costs to his neighbors (keeping a tree that might ruin his neighbor's breed), he is prone to overlook such things. Imposing a tax on the number of trees in an orchard helps correct thoughtless or careless behavior by encouraging owners to care for their property in ways that profit the community. An orchardist can do this by chopping down trees in his orchard that produce less than stellar bounty.

A question may be raised as to whether orchard owners *already* have incentives to chop down their poorly performing trees even in the absence of the tax. The answer is: maybe not. An orchard owner might be reluctant to sacrifice a mature, fruit-bearing tree for a young one that will not bear fruit for many more years. He may simply like a tree because it produces shade. Or he may be negligent, and fail to execute decisions that will be beneficial in the long term. *A tax makes it more likely that trees producing lower quality durian will be eliminated promptly and regularly.*

## Economics Lessons Using History

The purpose of memory, according to the clinical psychologist Jordan Peterson, is *not* to remember the past for its own sake, but to extract out lessons to structure the future. To a certain extent, similar claims can be made about the role of history. Note that the process of retelling a story or 'extracting out lessons' requires the editing out or dismissal of certain facts, details, and perspectives. The historian privileges certain aspects of his story over others. The loss in comprehensiveness and nuance may enhance a good story, one that is memorable and that offers key lessons that will be of future value.

Economists tend to be very comfortable boiling models down to their essence. The model of supply and demand, for instance, is so generic it is not uncommon to use the market for 'widgets', a hypothetical product the economics instructor doesn't bother to specify, to illustrate the workings of the model. Such tendencies can produce economic ideas that are logical and sharp, but overly simplistic and not entirely realistic. Historians, unlike most economists, possess an abundance of compelling stories. Compared to economic models, historical accounts tend to contain such nuance and complexity that drawing sharp insights to structure our understanding of the present and prepare for the future becomes very arduous or even impossible. The objective of the case studies in this volume is to construct a middle ground where students of economics and history can meet and benefit from each other's discipline. While the economist will profit from learning realistic and compelling stories from the past, the historian can gain an appreciation for the clear and precise insights of basic economic analysis.

The discussion of the durian orchard tax demonstrates what the reader can expect from the case studies in the following chapters. The durian case contains considerably more detail than is necessary in order to illustrate the economic concept of an external cost. The details, however, add context and realism to the application of an important economic idea in the real world, a feature that often goes missing in standard economic textbooks. For historians, the account is likely to come across as overly simplistic. Orchardists realized and practiced breed selection before the new tax came into their lives. Furthermore, the enforcement and consequences of the tax were much more complex and wide-ranging than what this short description offers. Yet, the lesson extracted from the simplified account is sharp and memorable. The trade-off has probably by now become clear. When reading these cases, economists are requested to accept additional messy realism in the application of their pristine models. Historians, in exchange, could temper some realism in their historical accounts to gain appreciation for sharp and portable economics concepts.

The history offered here and in the following chapters is not presented as definitive. These parables are only one of the many possible versions of the immense complexity of history. The accounts in each chapter are supported by the writings of serious and respected historians. Some may dispute the version of history you read here by offering distinct or even contradictory accounts. Most likely, other versions contain some, but not all, facets of the truth. It is the nature of history to acknowledge that every event is seen from multiple points of view, usually by conflicting protagonists. All the accounts may be in their own way accurate. Let it suffice to say here that while no single text can capture the whole truth, let us at least make the point we are able to present interesting.

## External Costs: A Modern Application

What are the lessons one can extract to better structure the future from the orchard tax case study? The global epidemic of antibiotic-resistant bacteria is a timely example.

Since their discoveries in the early twentieth century, antibiotics – drugs used to fight bacterial infections – have saved millions of lives and added over 20 years to the global average life expectancy. Simple infections that used to be life-threatening have become treatable with the discovery of these miracle drugs.

Unfortunately, many believe that humans have squandered this wonderful resource through constant misuse or overuse. Every time an antibiotic is used, bacteria in the environment are exposed to the drug, and while most may be killed, a few survive, develop a stronger resistance to the antibiotic, and pass on the resistance to descendants. Through an evolutionary, selection process, bacteria can develop complete resistance to an antibiotic after only a few generations of exposure. When someone is infected with this "super bug," his or her treatment options have thus been significantly narrowed.

It follows that when I take an antibiotic, I am imposing an external cost on members of my community through the increased risk of creating a mutant, a super bug that could then infect my neighbor, who would unexpectedly find himself out of treatment options. When individuals do not bear the external costs of their choices, they tend to make choices that needlessly generate excessive burdens on others. In this manner, individuals often seek antibiotics for trivial infections, the benefits for which are small. But the long-term costs of these behaviors are potentially very high. Given that the rate of new antibiotic discoveries is slowing, while the rate at which germs are mutating is accelerating, public health authorities are becoming gravely concerned that our stock of effective antibiotics will soon be depleted, a truly scary prospect.

The challenge of antibiotic-resistant germs, in many ways, resembles the durian breeding problem of the early nineteenth-century Siam. In the case of durian, an orchard owner did not fully consider the external cost imposed on his neighbors when leaving an inferior breed on his property. Only when a tax was imposed did he take a more socially responsible action. In the case of antibiotics, a person fails to take into account the danger he inflicts on others when taking antibiotics carelessly. The analogous solution is thus to impose a tax on antibiotics. That way, each time I feel unwell, I will deliberate more carefully about whether I really need a dose of *expensive* antibiotics. Perhaps, simply drinking lots of liquids and getting plenty of rest would suffice.

In essence, the scope of the impact of our individual choices varies considerably. Certain choices, such as how many lobes of durian to consume in one sitting, are entirely private. As long as you pay for the durian, the way you eat it is your business (unless you are a page serving in Vajiravudh's court, that is). The market price you pay for your indulgence ensures that you make measured choices. If the durian harvest is plentiful and cheap, feel free to indulge. If the harvest is poor, the steep price tag will encourage you to assess whether you would rather save your durian budget to indulge on something else – say, a massage. In other circumstances, like whether to take antibiotics when feeling unwell, your choice may impose a cost on innocent bystanders. The price you pay for the antibiotics covers the production and marketing costs of the producer. Yet, it fails to reflect the risk you contribute by hastening the emergence of a super bug that could claim many future lives. Because the choice about whether you will take antibiotics is no longer a strictly private decision, the government, representing the best interest of the majority, is justified in promulgating laws that make everyone's drugs more expensive.

Taxing life-saving drugs is an idea significantly less palatable than taxing nineteenth-century durian orchard owners, especially when we are reminded that the poor are also often in need of such medications. There are more subtle ways of making these drugs more costly in practice. Requiring antibiotics to be purchased by prescription is one such way. Obtaining a prescription requires a visit to a licensed physician, a trip that demands both time and a budget. The overall cost of obtaining antibiotics is significantly increased when a prescription is required. Regulations such as these are likely designed with public safety as a priority. The rules are intended to provide important safeguards for drug usage safety. Nevertheless, a quintessential hallmark of stricter regulations is higher prices, a consequence not dissimilar to that of imposing a tax, though the increase price goes to the doctors making the prescriptions and the pharmacists who dispense them rather than the government.

The preceding discussion suggests that examining economic practices in history (e.g., the orchard tax) can lead us into policy debates relevant in today's world (e.g., public health policy). As the analysis progresses, political and moral issues may emerge. For example, while some readers may see it as reasonable to ask individuals to pay their own medical bills, other readers may believe that it makes sense for the general vitality of the state that basic healthcare be made accessible to poor citizens as well as rich ones. For some, this discussion about drug pricing is wrong from the beginning. As with most parts of this volume, the ideas and insights should not be taken uncritically. While conclusions from basic economic analysis are neither universally palatable, nor wholly practical, they do introduce new ways of thinking that are potentially useful for grappling with a wide-range of important social problems. So, remember to keep an open mind, and enjoy the ride!

## Glossary of Economic Terms

**External cost**    a cost born by a third party or bystander who is *not* involved in the production, distribution, and consumption of a good or service.

## Note

1 Sixteen hundred square meters.

# 2  Incentives

## The Rise and Decline of Tax Farming in Early Bangkok

> *Relevant period*: 1767–1892 (Thonburi to early Bangkok)
> *Economic concepts*: principal-agent framework, sunk cost, adverse selection, moral hazard, rent seeking

In 1858, King Mongkut of Siam (Rama IV) was suffering some unusual anxiety. Over the past few years, Bun-long,[1] his trusted Minister of Lands (*Krom Na*) had deposited bonuses of more than a quarter million baht in His Majesty's Privy Purse. Because the money had been raised from land taxes, mainly charges on the Kingdom's thriving paddy cultivation, Mongkut was worried that his minister's largess would later stir controversy over inappropriate use of tax revenues.

To shield Bun-long from possible legal troubles, the King declared that any future complaints about the mishandling of funds from *Krom Na* would not be entertained. Such immunity was justified in Mongkut's eyes because Bun-long had always fulfilled all his ministerial financial obligations. Under Bun-long, *Krom Na* had each year furnished the royal granaries with sufficient quantities of rice and executed the usual sponsorship of royal monasteries. The minister had also dutifully sent the Treasury *16,000* baht every year – an amount *double* what previous heads of *Krom Na* had been capable of delivering. What Bun-long presented to the King for his personal use was therefore merely the excess. Bun-long performed his duties of supervising tax collection with utmost diligence.

Apart from evoking a grimace or a smile, this historical anecdote raises a few intriguing issues. Students of politics – noting the King's apprehension about the propriety of his own financial affairs – might debate the practical limits of the King's powers under the theoretical "absolute monarchy." This question would be appropriate for an entirely different discussion. Alternatively, those interested in business and economics would surely take note of the value of a 'diligent' subordinate. Apart from doubling *Krom Na*'s annual contribution to the Treasury, the industrious Bun-long had

DOI: 10.4324/9781003392262-2

consistently produced a sizeable bonus for his boss! The value of a talented and hard-working employee is no less important today. Imagine how much more profitable a modern corporation could be if its employees were similarly focused and committed to their tasks.

The following discussion will illustrate how employee selection, monitoring and motivation were problems as pertinent in nineteenth-century Siam as they are today. To fully appreciate the historical parallels with today's business challenges, we will introduce some precise vocabulary to describe general patterns of human behavior and interactions. Such vocabulary, while abstract and technical, will allow us to recognize recurring, general social phenomena. We will see that success or failure of solutions applied to past problems can provide useful insights for dealing with similar challenges of the modern world.

## Economy and Taxation at the Dawn of Bangkok

The glorious 417-year history of the Kingdom of Ayutthaya came to a violent demise in 1767 when the capital was sacked by its arch rival, the Burmese. The sacking left the Siamese economy in ruins. Taksin, governor of the northern province of Tak, emerged as a leading strongman determined to establish a new Siamese kingdom. He quickly founded his own capital in Thonburi, a small town which still thrives today on the West Bank of the Chao Phraya River. During the first year of Taksin's reign, more of his people starved to death than all those killed in the war with Burma. To sustain his struggling colony, Taksin cobbled together his resources and managed to import rice to feed his people. Siam's tributary trade with China was revived. Foreign trade was no longer a display of the King's glory as in the Ayutthaya period. It had become a means of survival.

While successful at unifying his kingdom and stabilizing the economy, Taksin did not see a peaceful ending to his reign. After ruling for 15 years, he was executed during a coup by Thongduang, one of his top generals, who then moved the capital across the Chao Phraya River from Thonburi to Bangkok. Crowning himself Rama I, the general became, in 1782, the first king of the Chakri dynasty.

Rama I adopted economic strategies similar to those of Taksin, utilizing trade as a tool to rebuild the economy. Significantly, the Ayutthaya tradition of reserving overseas commerce as a monopoly of the crown was abandoned, and patrician families were encouraged to also engage in trade. The thinking was that by allowing the nobles to more deeply involve themselves in commerce, they perhaps would be able to shoulder some of their own expenses instead of always relying on the royal purse.

By the early nineteenth century, a sustained peace across the Chao Phraya central plain fueled a boom in paddy cultivation. The aristocracy by now had grown increasingly business-savvy. Taking advantage of the blossoming economy, they soon eclipsed the crown in international trade. The royal merchant marine could no longer compete. There was also more competition in seagoing commerce from immigrant Chinese. Toward the end of the reign of Rama II, swelling palace expenditures coupled with faltering income from sea trade resulted in the treasury's reserves being badly depleted.

Ascending to the throne in 1824, King Rama III conceived a solution to his predecessor's financial woes. With a thriving economy, there was no longer a need for the palace itself to directly engage in trade. Instead, the King would harness the flourishing economy by taxing the successful commercial activities. However, collecting taxes called for a much more extensive bureaucratic apparatus. Residing in Bangkok, the King would need to rely on provincial governors to collect and deliver to him their local tax proceeds. As we have seen in the opening anecdote involving Bun-long, the amounts actually delivered could turn out to be both arbitrary and capricious. Where might the King find capable and diligent agents to work as tax collectors?

## The Principal-Agent Framework

The principal-agent framework is widely used in economics as a tool to analyze transactions in which one party (the 'principal') employs another party (the 'agent') to execute certain tasks on the former's behalf. Today, this framework might describe the relationship between a business owner and her employee. It is also a good model for understanding the modern corporation, where shareholders (the "owners") hire a CEO to run the company on their behalf. Back in the early days of Bangkok, the principal-agent framework would approximate the relationship between the King (the principal) and his officialdom (his agents).

It is not uncommon for the interest of the principal and the agent to be incongruent. In the case of a modern corporation, shareholders may want their CEO to run the business in such a way as to maximize the long-term value of the company. The CEO, on the other hand, may have her eyes on extra executive perks and improving her prospects of getting appointed to an even more lucrative position in the future. Contractual agreements can resolve such conflicts of interest by clearly specifying the terms of engagement between the two parties, e.g., how many hours of *work* the CEO is required to engage in per week. Complications arise, however, when the two parties have highly unequal amounts of information. For example, it might be unclear to an outsider whether the CEO playing a round of golf with potential clients should count as work. Under such settings, verifying and enforcing the terms of the contract are either prohibitively expensive or outright impossible.

In contract theory, asymmetric information problems come in two flavors, namely, the *hidden attributes* problem and *hidden actions* problem. We shall illustrate these two problems using the tax reform dilemma facing Rama III.

To increase his reliance on taxes as a source of state revenue, the King needed to depend on the governors he appointed to rule distant provinces.

These agents would be responsible for monitoring and collecting taxes on key economic activities including agricultural production, mining, gathering of forest goods, and distant land and maritime trade. It is not unreasonable to assume that provincial governors had very good information about the types and magnitudes of economic activities taking place in their territories. In fact, the King often appointed cooperative, well-connected local nobility as governors, who were expected to use their royally bestowed positions to live off their domains. It was thus in a governor's own best interest to gather information and track the growth of local trade so he could skim off an appropriate amount for himself.

Nevertheless, it is unreasonable to expect the governors to truthfully share with the King their private information about the true attributes of the local economy and the actual amounts of taxes they were collecting. With access to the full extent of this information, the King would have been in a position to demand a sizeable share of the proceeds. A superior strategy for each governor would be to keep the King in the dark about local production, to retain as much as he pleased from the tax revenue, and to surrender the remainder to the King, claiming that this residual was the most he and his people could muster, given the 'tepid local economy.' Unable to verify the truthfulness of the report, the King would have little choice but to accept whatever yearly amount he was offered. This unpalatable circumstance in which the King found himself had its origins in his information (or lack thereof) about the *attributes* of the local economy. The vital facts were available to the provincial governor (the "agent") but hidden from the King (the "principal").

It would be in the King's best interest if each governor took strong initiatives to boost tax revenues. Enterprising activities such as producing standardized clay pots for palm sugar and molasses would stimulate trade and thus bolster tax revenue from foodstuffs and pots. Policing to stamp out piracy and smuggling would boost production of island goods and birds' nests, which would in turn also increase tax revenues. Finally, remaining alert to emerging markets for which new taxes could be imposed, and initiating tax collection at the opportune moment would also benefit the royal purse.

While the King might wish to compel provincial governors to undertake such activities whenever possible, it seems unlikely that the governors would perform these tasks with utmost diligence. The work of carrying out initiatives would fall solely on the governor, but the resulting benefit would likely be shared between the governor and the King. When the party doing the hard work does not reap the full reward for his effort, we can usually expect the level of effort to be suboptimal (see the appendix for details). Because the King resides in Bangkok, a provincial governor cannot be closely monitored – the *hidden actions* problem. The governor can thus get away with shirking many of his duties toward the King.

Given these serious and endemic problems of *hidden attributes* and *hidden actions* within the principal-agent framework, there is little wonder why

King Mongkut was so surprised when his agent, Bun-long, bucked the trend and consistently produced for him exceptionally high annual land taxes. Apart from a one-off, happy coincidence of appointing a loyal and industrious agent like Bun-long, what strategies might the King use to increase the chances of obtaining higher performance from his tax collection agents?

## Tax Farming – A (Temporary) Silver Bullet

Tax farming is a unique method of tax collection dating back to the Roman era.[2] Records show that the system was also practiced in Siam during the late Ayutthaya period. The popularity of this system in early Bangkok was perhaps inspired by the Chinese. In essence, the system is based on outsourcing. The palace would outsource the engagement of a monopoly (e.g., gambling) or the collection of taxes to the entrepreneur who placed the highest bid for the job. The outsourcing contract specified a lump-sum payment to the palace (and the tax rate in the case of tax collection). These specifications essentially made the tax farmer the residual claimant of revenues beyond what the palace was promised. In addition to the efficiency benefits of this setup (as will become apparent later), the tax farming system also relieved the palace of significant bureaucratic burdens, had it been required to manage such operations itself. The competitive bidding process, together with the powerful incentives built into the system, contributed to the legendary success of the Treasury during the reign of King Rama III.

The tax farming system has the potential to overcome both the *hidden attributes* and the *hidden actions* problems. Let us begin with the latter. Economists imagine that individuals make choices based on an analysis of benefits and costs involved. An endeavor is undertaken only when the expected benefits exceed the costs. Not all costs, however, are the same. A key assumption about decision making under the benefit-cost framework is that the only benefits and costs that matter are those the decision maker can control *going forward.*

As an illustration, consider a merchant whose fleet of ships was just lost to a severe storm during an ambitious trading expedition. Should our merchant attempt to salvage the lost merchandise, or should he spend his remaining capital on other promising projects? A wise business advisor would undoubtedly recommend the latter. Putting to rest the merchandise on the ocean bed, taking stock, and making the best investments with his eyes firmly on the future would be the most sensible course of action for our merchant. The profits could then be used to recoup some of the losses before maybe taking on another expedition. *What has already been sunk is irrelevant for present decisions.*[3]

We can apply the same logic to an entrepreneurial tax farmer who has just won an auction to collect taxes on, say, palm sugar. His winning bid – the amount he must deliver to the Treasury – is analogous to merchandise that has already sunk to the bottom of the ocean. His current decisions and future actions should be based solely on forthcoming benefits and costs he can control. All tax proceeds that the tax farmer collects count as *his* benefits. He must weigh these benefits against all *future* costs, such as travel, lodging and helpers. The lump sum he agreed to pay the Treasury is sunk and thus irrelevant. The tax farmer will keep investing more time and effort in collecting taxes on palm sugar cultivation as long as the expected benefit from those efforts exceed the cost. Notice that such behavior is akin to that of a business owner, the business here being tax collection on palm sugar. There is no longer the problem of the tax collector shirking his duties.

Moreover, if the tax farmer expects to be in the business for the long haul,[4] he also faces proper incentives to make growth-promoting investments. Producing standardized clay pots for palm sugar and molasses were indeed activities often undertaken by the palm sugar tax farmer. Tax farmers in charge of bird nest collection regularly patrolled the caves to stave off smugglers. Again, the system incentivizes desirable behavior without any need for monitoring. In short, tax farming solves the *hidden actions problem* in tax collection by setting up proper incentives!

But how does the palace know the lump sum offered upfront by the tax farmer is an appropriate quantity given the revenues he will eventually procure? Such a question contains a flavor of the *hidden attributes problem*. A tax farmer candidate who is willing to stake his livelihood on the proceeds from certain taxes is likely to possess superior estimates of the attributes of the relevant markets and the expected amount of the final tax revenue. How can the palace bargain for a fair share of the earnings?

While candidate tax farmers are certain to shade their bids to ensure they earn some profits at the end of the day, it can be expected that, under certain circumstances, competition will prevent the bidders from slashing their bids by too much. Imagine an incumbent tax farmer who becomes too greedy and offers a particularly low bid for his continued tax-collection privilege. News of the submitted bid will quickly attract aspiring new tax farmers to try to outbid the incumbent. Sooner or later, the bidding war will push the lump sum payment to the government back up to levels pretty close to the expected size of the true tax revenue. Competition ameliorates the informational disadvantage of the palace.

The palace realized that the enterprising energies of the private sector could be harnessed for activities other than maritime trade. Growing political stability, together with a swelling population during the first three reigns of Bangkok, allowed domestic commerce to thrive. An expanded role for tax farming, in which enterprising entrepreneurs were recruited to help collect taxes from various commercial activities, helped the palace extract more resources from the flourishing domestic economy. As Rama III withdrew from the sea trade and focused on taxing, Treasury reserves grew. Commerce was booming and the palace was once again in a strong position to finance activities such as staging military expeditions and renovating Buddhist temples.

## Hidden Information Problems through Different 'World Views'

Let us end this section by considering the problem we originally set out to investigate – how can a principle select an honest and capable agent to best carry out certain tasks on her behalf? The table below delineates different worldviews on two desirables – honesty and conscientiousness. The *first worldview* sees these desirables as innate characters. According to this perspective, a moral person behaves honestly under all circumstances. Likewise, diligent people naturally act conscientiously when assigned a task. Because such attributes (moral character and dispositions) are often difficult to observe or verify, *selecting* an innately honest and diligent agent becomes the key challenge facing the principal. The hidden nature of such important attributes often results in the principal hiring a promising candidate only to later learn that the chosen agent lacks moral character and/or the desired disposition. Such poor outcomes due to a lack of accurate attributional information prior to making a decision is known in economics as the *adverse selection* problem.

|  |  | Desirables | |
| --- | --- | --- | --- |
|  |  | Honesty | Conscientiousness |
| World Views | Innate character drives behavior (Adverse Selection) | Honest behavior is a moral character | Conscientiousness is a disposition |
|  | Behavior Is Situational-Specific (Moral Hazard) | Close monitoring prevents dishonesty | Proper incentives prevent shirking |

In the *second worldview*, honesty and conscientiousness are both situational-specific – there are no inherently good or bad people. What this means is that an agent will behave honestly and perform her tasks conscientiously under the right circumstance. The 'right circumstance' here refers to when the agent is being monitored or given appropriate incentives. According to this second worldview, most people succumb to cheating when their actions take place behind closed doors. Similarly, shirking one's tasks predominantly arises from a lack of suitable incentives. The central problem facing the principle is therefore *not* in selecting the right agent but instead in properly monitoring the agent's actions and setting up the right reward and punishment mechanisms. When monitoring actions taken by the agent are expensive or difficult (which by definition makes accurate rewarding and punishing impossible), the ensuing cheating and/or shirking is, in economic jargon, referred to as *moral hazard*.

### Tax Farming and the Adverse Selection Problem

Tax farming is designed to solve the adverse selection problem, and the system can do so successfully under the right conditions. Competitive bidding for the right to collect taxes favors the most capable entrepreneur. The ability to collect more taxes lets the most efficient candidate outbid his competitors. Assuming the bidding is transparent and competitive (something one cannot always take for granted), the problem of selecting the most capable and diligent agent is thus resolved.

The system's ability to select for honesty is perhaps less interesting to analyze. An imposter could conceivably place a winning bid, collect the relevant taxes and fail to make the promised lump-sum payment. Such blatant cheating can probably be prevented by some simple screening to make sure bidders are credible. Ultimately, a fraudulent tax farmer who cheats on his contract with the King obviously does not have a long career ahead of him.

### Tax Farming and the Moral Hazard Problem

Appointing a tax farmer to take charge of tax collection does *not* heighten the King's ability to monitor his agent. Instead, the tax farming system resolves moral hazard by creating the right *incentives*. Once the right to collect a certain tax has been assigned, the tax farmer treats the enterprise as though it is his own. All *future* benefits and costs from his actions accrue to him. Therefore, shirking is no longer advantageous. The tax farmer will work diligently as it is in his own best interest to do so.

There is the possibility that a tax farmer exploits the King's subjects by tricking or coercing them into paying taxes at a rate higher than what was specified. Such conning would benefit the tax farmer by enlarging his receipts, while potentially generating popular unrest, to the King's detriment. This dishonest behavior would likely arise when the tax farmer is allowed to carry out his work without proper monitoring.

Avoiding exploitation of the citizenry requires close monitoring. The tax farmer, usually a Chinese entrepreneur, needs the cooperation of local officials to do his job. If the officials refuse to facilitate tax collection, the tax farmer cannot coerce the locals to surrender their dues. On the other hand, the local officials are expected to constrain the tax farmer to act within his rightful authorities. When a tax farmer attempts to exploit the populace by over taxing them, the local officials must stand up to prevent the injustice. During the early reigns of Bangkok, local officials harbored a healthy level of animosity toward tax farmers. Because the Chinese tax collectors were viewed as encroachers, local officials were steadfast allies of their citizens, effectively curtailing the tax farmer's ability to abuse his privileges. The moral hazard problem was thus kept in check.

## Rent Seeking and the Demise of Tax Farming

The success of tax farming hinges on two vital requirements – (i) a competitive bidding process to allocate tax farming rights, and (ii) the existence of strong local officials capable of preventing abuses of power by the tax farmers. Both requirements seemed to have been satisfied somewhat during the reign of Rama III. As pointed out earlier, local Siamese officials viewed the tax farmers with distrust and acted as checks against their abuse of power. The Chinese entrepreneurs were also not yet sufficiently organized to collude and rig the bidding process.

Tax farming became a less successful revenue-generating mechanism for the palace during subsequent reigns. As the Chinese tax farmers and local officials grew increasingly acquainted with each other, safeguards against the tax collectors' abuse of power became less effective. When local officials could be bribed to allow the tax farmer to overtax the peasants, ordinary citizens bore the brunt of the hardship. Of course, the peasantry always had the option of reverting to subsistence agriculture, and thereby completely avoid paying any taxes. Although there are records of some commercial production being taxed out of existence, such problems are unlikely to become endemic. Because the tax farmer holds a significant stake in commercial production, the shrewd businessman will be very careful not to kill the goose that lays the golden egg.

The more serious problem leading to the demise of tax farming was the breaking down of the competitive bidding system for tax farming rights. Toward the end of the reign of Rama IV, Chinese secret societies grew influential and began dominating the tendering process. Bidding was restricted to a small circle of well-connected businessmen. Under such circumstances, it became easier for the bidders to cooperate to ensure that the winning bid would promise only a small lump sum payment to the Treasury. When bidding was done under collusion, the profits of tax farmers swelled while revenues reaching the treasury dwindled.

The government's income from tax farming continued to diminish despite the King's decree establishing tax farming for 14 new items from fish and poultry to lotteries and entertainment troupes. The Crown's difficulties were also being exacerbated by new tariff restrictions imposed by the Bowring treaty, a trade liberalization agreement signed with the British in 1855 (see Chapter 3 for more discussion). Owing to these problems, King Rama V ascended to the throne inheriting treasury funds he considered inadequate.

The collusion between tax farmers and local officials and among the tax collectors themselves are activities referred to in economics as '*rent seeking.*' Rent seeking refers to self-enriching activities that create no additional value. When tax farmers and officials conspired to collude among themselves, they merely appropriated more resources for themselves at the expense of the government and the productive sector, namely the peasants. A society that allows its rent-seeking sector to grow unchecked will experience low productivity and high levels of inequality. The economy's productive sector will also suffer from harmful distortions as substantial resources have to be deployed to evade extortion by rent-seekers.

King Rama V was well aware of the serious problems that had become ingrained in the tax farming system. He resented the financial clout of the Chinese tax farmers, which he believed could pose a political threat to his reform policies. Throughout the late nineteenth century, the King passed numerous regulations to more closely control tax farming. Responsibility for collecting taxes was gradually transferred to government bureaucrats. By 1892, the government had made a commitment to undertake all commodity tax collection, with the exception of the monopolies for opium, liquor, and lotteries, which would continue to be managed by tax farmers. The newly created Ministry of Interior would be responsible for collecting such taxes in the provinces.

Considering just the incentive structures, having salaried bureaucrats collect taxes instead of tax farmers is likely to yield smaller revenues for the Treasury. This expectation arises due to the fact that salaried officials did not enjoy the potent incentives of being a residual claimant of tax collection activity like tax farmers did. As collection was transferred to officials, the King did in fact witness reductions in revenue. In fact, many Chinese businessmen made successful petitions to reclaim their collection responsibilities and they paid the government much more than what was being collected by bureaucrats. Such reversions, however, were infrequent and short-lived. By the early twentieth century, the tax farming system in Siam had largely wound down and was no longer operating.

## Epilogue: Is Outsourcing a Solution for Organizational Information Problems?

Employing an outside party to take charge of an organizational function is known in management jargon as *outsourcing*. Modern corporations regularly outsource numerous functions to external partners. Functions commonly outsourced include information technology, customer service, facilities management, marketing and advertising, and legal documentation. From this perspective, tax farming can be viewed as a move by the government to out-source tax collection.

Like any other economic decision, the outsourcing choice is based on a benefit-cost calculation. The key benefit of outsourcing is efficiency. Eliminating an internal department, be it IT, legal or facilities management, frees the corporation from having to select, monitor and motivate departmental staff – tasks that are fraught with *adverse selection* and *moral hazard*. When service providers submit bids for an outsourcing contract, competitive pressure will favor the most efficient bidder. As competitive auctions for tax farming rights helped the palace maximize tax revenues, bidding for outsourcing contracts helps corporations maximize the value gained from their spending on procuring a functional service. Outsourcing also frees the corporation from the costs of monitoring and incentivizing a subset of its staff because these expenses are now on the outsourcing partner's payroll.

Other well-known benefits of outsourcing include economies of scale and learning. A service provider can aggregate the demand for a given service across many client firms. The larger the operation of a service provider, the greater the potential benefits from economies of scale. Savings accruing from larger size (economies of scale) often arise from the ability to spread fixed costs across more output units. A facilities management company, for example, may be able to use the same software for all of its clients, making the average cost of service go down with each additional client. A service provider's experience and expertise also give it an advantage from economies of learning. The greater the experience an outsourcing partner has accumulated, the more likely the partner will be able to provide high quality service at a competitive price.

Not all functions are outsourced because insourcing can also offer important advantages. The key benefits of insourcing (i.e., what a firm must forego if it chooses to outsource) include superior coordination and more secure control of critical resources. Firms that base their competitive advantage on safety standards such as those in the food industry may be reluctant to outsource parts of their supply chain due to concerns about industry standards and hygiene. Technology companies may also choose not to outsource in order to protect their proprietary technology and knowledge. To outsource or insource is therefore an exercise in weighing the benefits and costs of each option.

## Glossary of Economic Terms

**Principal-agent framework**   a tool to analyze transactions in which one party (the 'principal') employs another party (the 'agent') to execute certain tasks on the former's behalf. It is not uncommon that the interest of the principal and the agent are incongruent, leading to difficulties in the relationship.

**Sunk cost**   a cost that has already been paid and will be difficult or impossible to recover. Decision makers would do best to ignore these costs when making decisions for the future.

**Adverse selection**   a lack of accurate attributional information prior to making a decision resulting in poor outcomes. Adverse selection is one class of information asymmetry problems arising when the parties in a transaction possess unequal information on what is being transacted.

**Moral hazard**   the cheating and/or shirking that often follows when monitoring actions taken by the agent are expensive or difficult. Moral hazard is another information asymmetry problem arising when the parties in a transaction possess unequal information on actions taken after the contract agreement.

**Rent seeking**   self-enriching activities that create no additional value.

# Appendix

## The Relationship between Effort and Reward

In this chapter, we postulated that, in the principal-agent framework, one important cause underlying the moral hazard problem was insufficient incentives for the agent. In this appendix, we will investigate the benefit-cost calculations of the agent more analytically, and, in the process, illustrate more clearly how the tax farming system may help lessen moral hazard.

Figure 2.1 graphically illustrates the benefit-cost analyses of an effortful task – for concreteness let us make it collecting taxes on sugar cane. The horizontal axis measures the percentage of total cane cultivation area visited by the tax collector. The vertical axis measures the value of the tax collected *and* the costs incurred by the tax collector, both in monetary terms. The slope of the cost of effort graph starts out flat but then becomes increasingly steep. This

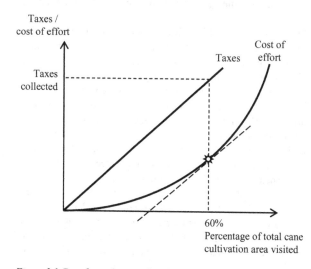

*Figure 2.1* Benefits and costs when the tax collector keeps all the proceeds

feature reflects the assumption that the marginal cost of effort is increasing as the collector is required to visit increasingly remote and inaccessible areas, once the easily reached fields have all been called upon. The other upward-sloping line labeled "Taxes" shows the relationship between the percentage of cane cultivation area visited and the amount of taxes collected. For simplicity, we assume the relationship is linear.

Let us begin by assuming the tax collector can keep all the proceeds for himself. In deciding what percentage of cane cultivation area to visit, the tax collector compares the marginal benefit and marginal cost of his effort, the benefit here simply being the tax revenues. The *marginal* benefit is the slope (or the steepness) of the benefit line. Similarly, the marginal cost is the slope of the 'Cost of effort' curve. It makes sense for the tax collector to keep increasing the percent of total cane cultivation area visited as long as the slope of the benefit line (or the marginal benefit) exceeds the slope of the 'Cost of effort' curve (or marginal cost). The slopes of the two coincide at 60% of total cane cultivation area visited. To the left of this point, the marginal benefits exceed the marginal costs. To the right of this point, the marginal costs exceed the marginal benefits. The tax collector thus chooses to visit three-fifths of all taxable cane cultivation area during the tax collection season. The total amount of taxes collected is represented by the height of the 'Taxes' line at 60% cultivation area visited.

Now consider the scenario in which the tax collector is an agent working for his principal. The principal and agent must agree on a share of the tax proceeds. Let us assume that the agent gets a 10% cut, with the remaining going to the principal.

Figure 2.2 illustrates the agent's benefit-cost calculations under the new circumstances. In this case, the slope of the agent's benefit has become much flatter. Using the same logic as that used in Figure 2.1, the agent tax collector will continue visiting more cultivation area as long as the slope of the revenue line (the marginal revenue) exceeds the slope of the total cost line (the marginal cost). In Figure 2.2, the slopes of the benefit and cost lines coincide at 25% of total cultivation. Beyond this point, the agent's marginal benefit, or 10% of the additional taxes, does not justify the agent's cost of effort. Total revenue collected is far lower compared to Figure 2.1, because the tax collector (the agent) is no longer willing to travel great distances to visit taxable sugarcane fields and spend more time haggling with uncooperative peasants.

Recalling our discussion about the irrelevance of sunk cost, one then realizes that the tax farmer's calculations resemble those of Figure 2.1. Moreover, since the total surplus (taxes minus cost of effort) is bigger in Figure 2.1, it is possible to specify a lump-sum payment from the agent to the principal in such a way that both sides are better off, compared to what they were experiencing in Figure 2.2.

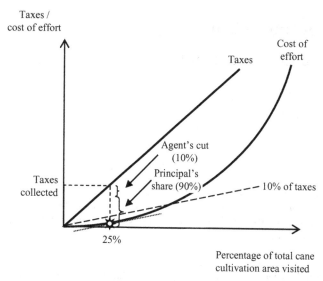

*Figure 2.2* Benefits and costs when the agent keeps 10% of the proceeds

In solving the moral hazard problem, the tax farming system (under the right circumstance) can end up making both the King and his tax collectors better off.

## Notes

1 Phraya Phonlathep (Long Bun-long).
2 Saint Matthew, chosen by Jesus, as a disciple, was a tax collector, and probably a tax farmer.
3 The inability to let go of what has already been lost, and allowing those losses to influence present decisions is famously known as the *sunk cost fallacy*. Over-eating at an all-you-can eat buffet or trudging through a book you've found to be awful since Chapter 1 are perhaps relatable examples of this decision-making fallacy.
4 Such expectations would seem reasonable as the incumbent tax farmer enjoys considerable advantages, (such as superior local information, industry knowledge, and business connections) over a newcomer. Challenging the incumbent in a tax farming auction is often a poor bet.

# 3    Globalization

## The Economics of Corvée

*Relevant period*: 1782–1868 (early Bangkok)
*Economic concepts*: opportunity cost, marginal product of labor, specific factors model, equilibrium, substitutes, complements, nominal and real wages

Agrarian-based societies have long occupied the Chao Phraya River basin, home to the capital of Siam or modern-day Thailand. The intensity of agricultural cultivation was low up to the early nineteenth century. Because most of the terrain was either swamp or dense forests, cultivation was limited to narrow strips of land along river banks. Rice, the region's food staple, was grown primarily for subsistence and to support the occasional appetite of elites for military expeditions.

Hunting and gathering were equally important to the economy. For domestic consumption and trade, wild hinterlands offered a rich supply of forest goods such as venison and deer hide, timber, spices, and herbs that were used both for domestic consumption and trade. Kings vied for control over the trading routs of these products to expand their economic influence and extract tariffs. The forest goods were an important part of the palace's highly profitable trade with China.

A tributary system set the protocol for trade with China. Within this imperial scheme, Siam acted as a vassal state of the Chinese empire. Siamese rulers would send 'tribute' to the Chinese emperor, who would then reciprocate with his own handsome gifts. While the practice was shrouded in myths of power and glory, it was often manipulated for profit. In practice, tributary exchange soon evolved into a system of lucrative gaming, albeit one monopolized by the royals. However, the palace's domination of Sino-Siamese trade gradually declined during the early decades of Bangkok, as the aristocracy and immigrant Chinese merchants captured more and more of the lucrative maritime trade. However, the Siamese kings eventually ceased to rely on international trade as their primary source of income, turning to taxation of the growing economy to raise most of the essential revenue.

DOI: 10.4324/9781003392262-3

The low intensity of agriculture kept the size of the population in check. Estimates for the early nineteenth century put the total number of people living in Bangkok and the agricultural central plain at around half a million. The sparse population made control of labor the key factor in determining political power. Siamese rulers developed a corvée system, forcing male commoners to work for the palace or noble households for six months out of every year. During times of peace, corvée labor was used for palace chores, digging moats, and repairing city walls. During times of war, these conscripts became foot soldiers.

The corvée system was not completely uncontested. Many commoners resented being forced into servitude and fled to the forests to avoid conscription. The strategic importance of labor drove the elites to invent increasingly harsh measures to combat the problem of men trying to escape. For example, during the early years of Bangkok the king ordered all male commoners to have their wrists tattooed as evidence of corvée registration. Those who escaped, known as "white wrists," were severely punished if caught.

Commoners who chose to comply with corvée registration found some advantages – mainly in the protection of rights and property under the law. Those who registered were left to till their land without harassment during the cultivation season. After the harvest, the women took over the responsibilities of caring for the farm and family as the men departed for their extended corvée service. This practice remained in place until the mid-nineteenth century, when the forces of globalization transformed the traditional Siamese economy. As it became more market-based and more intensely agrarian, the corvée was rendered untenable.

## Colonialism and Globalization

When the British in the early 1840s defeated China in the Opium War, the profitable trade between Siam and China sharply declined, and trade with Europe gradually replaced it. The imperialists were eager to buy foodstuffs – mainly rice – from Siam to sustain their Asian colonies in India, Ceylon, Malaya, and Java, all of which had been brought under systems of cash-crop[1] plantation. The Siamese elite were keen to trade rice for modern weaponry and exotic Western goods. Bigger and more efficient European ships facilitated a rapid expansion of Bangkok as an East-West commercial center in Southeast Asia. The pace of *globalization* rapidly accelerated.

For the purposes of this discussion, globalization refers, in particular, to a growing integration of cross-border production and consumption. Colonial cash-crop plantations, focused on large-scale agricultural production for export while other domestic needs of the colonized peoples were to be satisfied by imports. This is a prime example of the globalization that emerged in the mid-nineteenth century. It was largely driven by colonialism. Improved transport in the form of powerful steamships and railways represented the hardware in this process. The theoretical justification of so-called free-trade conceived decades earlier by economists such as Adam Smith and David Ricardo served as the software driving these operations.

There was an annoying pebble in the commercial shoe of the Europeans, however, i.e., Siam's tariff collection procedures. Western merchants found the tariffs imposed at the port of Bangkok to be erratic, repetitive, excessive, and often irritatingly unfair. European traders, for example, were often required to trade with the king at disadvantageous terms before they could do business with the locals. Furthermore, tariffs and fees that were actually charged did not match the rates that had been announced. Such inequities, when imposed by the Siamese, were viewed as a hindrance to free-trade ideals.[2]

In 1855, Sir John Bowring, the British governor of Hong Kong, sailed up the Chao Phraya River with a fleet of war ships to negotiate a trade treaty. The resulting agreement, famously known as the *Bowring Treaty*, stipulated that British merchants could trade freely in all ports of Siam and enjoy a fixed, non-duplicate, tariff rate of 3%. The treaty was signed under the shadow of British military might in the context of colonial expansion, and it contained stipulations unpalatable to Siamese rulers. Even so, the ensuing liberalization went a long way in stimulating Bangkok's economic activity and growth, especially in the production and export of rice.

Such sustained growth in trade, however, would not have been possible under severe limitations of labor and arable land. Two concurrent developments helped ease these historic constraints.

First, the region's population began to increase significantly, beginning in the early nineteenth century. The swelling labor pool resulted from growing numbers of war captives and voluntary migrants such as traders and laborers from China. Second, the escalating demand for rice spurred Siamese elites to initiate various canal projects to drain the massive swamps of the Central Plain, thereby converting areas that were previously under water into agricultural land. The canals – the ones crossing the Rangsit tract north of Bangkok being the most notable – were also used as transportation routes, further enhancing commercial prospects.

Though they had extensive experience controlling labor, Siamese nobles lacked experience in leasing or renting property. Competition for the new land along the canals became intense as commoners were quick to stake claims giving little heed to formal property titles. In spite of the disarray, virtually every square inch of the central basin was eventually converted into paddy.

The nature of agricultural production in the region was being profoundly transformed. As agriculture changed from subsistence to intensive, the prominence of trade and export grew. Between the 1860s and 1930s, the total annual amount of Siamese rice being shipped abroad grew from around 100,000 tons to 1.5 million tons.[3]

## Productivity, Opportunity Costs, and the Specific Factors Model

As paddy cultivation intensified, labor shortages became severe. Land is a major factor of production, and it was becoming more plentiful, thanks to irrigation projects. Then, however, the demand for the other necessary factor of production – labor – also started to increase. At the same time, the old corvée system continued to call for conscripts. Who would win in this tug-of- war for manpower?

Economic theory predicts that a factor of production will flow to the sector in which it will be most productive. Two concurrent developments suggest that, in early nineteenth-century Siam, agrarian labor was much more productive than corvée. First, expanding arable land allowed farmers to grow more rice. Suitable cultivation techniques were taking full advantage of large, fertile fields, and output per worker in the lower Chao Phraya Basin was among the highest in the region. Second, growing demand for rice exports meant that this output was rising in value. Together, these two developments made working in the agrarian sector highly attractive.

As paddy fields now promised much more ample rewards, corvée conscription was increasingly regarded as extremely burdensome. In economics, the sacrifice one must make to pursue a choice is referred to as the *opportunity cost*. Prior to the rice boom, male commoners had few opportunities outside the normal cultivation season. Under that circumstance, tolerating the opportunity cost of corvée had seemed bearable, considering the high price of not being registered. However, with more arable land and improved irrigation,[4] corvée service now meant foregoing significant opportunities for productive work in the fields. The rising market price of paddy greatly increased the opportunity cost of being conscripted. The forces of globalization were undercutting the viability of Siam's corvée system by escalating the opportunity cost of conscription.

To better visualize the relationship between productivity and the mobility of labor among different economic sectors, we will examine the famous *Specific Factors Model*. Although they require an oversimplification of the real world, models can sharpen our comprehension of the underlying forces of real-world phenomena that are often obscured by the details and complexities of social interactions. A good model is also portable, meaning it can be counted upon to yield insights in diverse situations across geography and time.

In the model we are constructing, we imagine two sectors of the Siamese economy during the mid-nineteenth century – the sector that instituted and operated the corvée and the agrarian sector. The elite who controlled the corvée determined the productive activities within that system. Male commoners were obligated to supply six months of labor each year to work on public projects, including warfare, or serve in the household of a noble family. During their six months of relative freedom, peasants engage in subsistence farming, and hunting and gathering. Sector-specific capital in the sector controlled by the elite included corvée registries, servants' quarters in residences of the elite, equipment, and facilities for punishing escapees, and weaponry used to wage war.

Commoners who evaded corvée to devote their labor to agricultural production were part of the second sector, which we call the peasantry. They employed numerous strategies to elude servitude, each associated with a different risk of getting caught and punished. A commoner could bribe officials, arrange to become somebody's slave in order to gain exemption from corvée, fake insanity, or simply flee to the forests. The peasantry also possesses sector-specific capital such as irrigation systems, farming equipment, and means for transporting crops.

Capital is sector-specific, but labor can move from one sector to another. In other words, an indentured servant could flee his master to work on a farm while a corvée escapee could turn himself in for registration. A sector that experiences a growing number of workers will be capable of generating more output – magnificent palaces and war loot in the case of the elite- controlled sector and rice in the case of the peasantry.

Production in both sectors, however is subject to the economic law of *decreasing marginal productivity*. Specifically, when the amount of capital is fixed, each new worker added to the labor force will be capable of generating less and less additional output. For example, suppose that increasing the number of foot soldiers from 1,000 to 1,001 men would gain an additional 1 oz of gold per year looted during military expeditions. But going from 5,000 to 5,001 men would be likely to augment the quantity of loot by a smaller amount, say ½ oz of gold per year. The decreasing benefit from adding more men to an army may be due to the poorer quality of weaponry when the military gets excessively large, or to the simple fact that profitable warfare opportunities are limited. Figure 3.1 graphically illustrates the concept of decreasing marginal productivity.

What do the assumptions of *mobile labor* and *decreasing marginal productivity* suggest about the quantity of employment and output in these two sectors? Economists like to think that a natural balance – an equilibrium – will emerge in such a way that neither sector employs too many workers. What does "too many" mean here? An example best explains the point.

Suppose there are 6,000 workers in the economy, with 5,001 employed in corvée labor and 999 corvée-escapees living as peasants. For simplicity, assume that corvée labor is devoted entirely to looting neighboring states while peasants are engaged exclusively in rice growing. According to Figure 3.1, if the number of foot soldiers dropped from 5,001 to 5,000, the total quantity of looted gold would fall by half an ounce each year. On the other hand, if an additional laborer added to the pool of 999 peasants could increase the annual rice output by one ton a year, and an ounce of gold traded for a ton of rice,

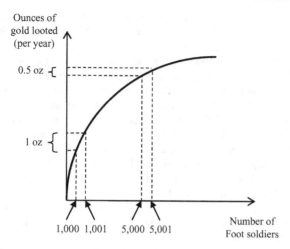

*Figure 3.1* Decreasing marginal productivity of labor – corvée sector

then economists would declare that "too many" workers were being absorbed by the corvée.

The logic behind this claim is that a transfer of one laborer from corvée to the peasantry would result in a loss of ½ oz of gold annually from looting, but a gain of one additional ton of rice per year from farming is worth 1 oz of gold. On net, the economy gains additional value worth ½ oz of gold, so the transfer is beneficial. In other words, there are too many workers in the corvée and too few in the peasantry. Labor could therefore profitably flow from the less productive sector to the more productive one.

As long as there can be beneficial transfers of workers from one sector to another, the economy is not in equilibrium. Equilibrium can be attained only when the marginal productivity of labor – the incremental output gained by adding one more worker to the sector – is equalized in both sectors.

In reality, why might we expect labor to relocate from a sector with too many workers to another sector with too few workers? The short answer is that when there is benefit to be had, enterprising individuals will sooner or later figure out a way to access it. Coming back to our example, a Siamese noble, observing the low quantity of loot delivered per foot soldier, might bribe a palace official for the opportunity to use corvée labor to work on his own paddy fields.

Occasionally, someone did notice that men could be so much more productive on paddy fields than in battle fields. The noble and the parole officer typically arrived at a mutually beneficial deal. Commoners were given the option of making a commutation payment in lieu of their corvée labor. As the market economy expanded, more and more men chose to make the payment and avoid conscription. Clearly, there were growing opportunities for able bodies to increase their income.

Figure 3.2 graphically illustrates the concept of equilibrium in the Specific Factors Model. The horizontal axis represents the total amount of labor in the economy. The downward sloping lines – from left to right for the corvée sector and from right to left for the peasantry – denote the decreasing marginal productivity of labor (MPL) in the two sectors. To make the marginal productivities ($MPL_C$ and $MPL_P$, where the subscripts C and P stand for "corvée" and "peasant" respectively) comparable, we multiply each quantity by the price of the output in each sector, namely $P_G$ or the price of "gold" from looting (baht per oz), and $P_R$ or the price of rice from farming (baht per ton). The crossing of the two lines – where the marginal values of labor in both sectors coincide – indicates the equilibrium of labor allocation between the two sectors. Notice that the intersection identifies on the horizontal axis the shares of labor working in each sector.

Here comes the payoff for the patience we have invested in building this model. What does the model indicate will happen in Siam's labor market in the face of the arising forces of globalization? First, growing demand for rice from the European colonists exerted upward pressure on the price of

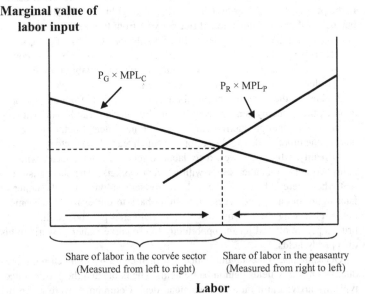

Figure 3.2 Equilibrium in the specific factors model

rice ($P_R \Rightarrow P_R^*$). The expanding amount of arable land due to the numerous canal projects also raised the marginal productivity of peasant labor ($MPL_P \Rightarrow MPL_P^*$) because with more land available an additional body can be more productive. Together, these changes resulted in an upward shift of the line representing the marginal value of labor for the peasantry (the line sloping from right to left). The shift expands the peasant workforce at the expense of the corvée. As more workers evade corvée to work in paddy fields, the marginal productivity of labor (MPL) in both sectors increases. Eventually, a new equilibrium is reached at a new intersection – the agricultural sector expands at the expense of the corvée sector. Figure 3.3 graphically illustrates these changes.

Historical events support the insights gleaned from the model. First, corvée evasion intensified as the rice trade expanded in the late nineteenth and early twentieth centuries. In 1855, King Mongkut (Rama IV) was deeply frustrated by the low numbers reported in a royal corvée registration. Bangkok's military campaigns mostly faltered after the mid-nineteenth century due to a lack of foot soldiers. The marginal productivity of labor also appeared to have increased significantly, as the model predicts. The average rice production per person grew by more than 100 kilograms between the mid-nineteenth and the mid-twentieth centuries.

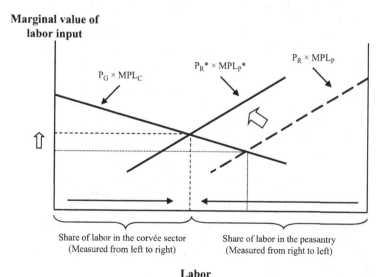

*Figure 3.3* The effects of increases in available land and the price of rice

## Substitutes, Complements, and the Transformation from Unfree to Free Labor

Globalization involves not only the cross-border movement of goods but also of people. In the nineteenth century, rapid population growth and decaying institutions drove China under the Qing Dynasty into political instability and famine. Tens of thousands of Chinese annually voyaged across the oceans to Siam, many choosing to settle down and adopt her as their new home. By the turn of the century, between four and six hundred thousand Chinese immigrants were living in Siam.

This influx helped ease the labor shortage in Bangkok. In standard economic jargon, immigrant Chinese labor acted as a *substitute* for corvée labor. The government's need for labor could be eased by hiring coolies. Having arrived in a new land with little more than *a pillow and a mat*,[5] Chinese immigrants were eager to take up any opportunities to make a living. Public works requiring hard labor such as digging canals and erecting and maintaining the city's infrastructure were completed for the most part by Chinese labor. Locals, eager to work the land outside of the city walls, paid a tax to evade corvée.

The most enterprising members of the Chinese immigrant community quickly accumulated funds to lift themselves out of the laboring class. With their hard-earned savings, they built mills, became traders, and even founded shipping businesses to facilitate the booming rice trade. Such entrepreneurial Chinese businessmen acted as important *complements* to the local agrarian labor. Milling, shipping, and trading services made the paddy grown by local farmers more valuable.

Vice versa, the more paddy farmers were able to grow, the more the businesses of the urban Chinese thrived. In this sense, local peasantry and burgeoning Chinese business helped reinforce each other and generated, over time, mutual benefits.

*Substitutes* and *complements* are recurrent concepts in economics. In the modern labor market, we often hear claims that robots and artificial intelligence will gradually substitute for human labor. To some extent, such substitution has already happened – think ATMs replacing bank tellers and automatic checkout counters replacing supermarket cashiers. Less frequently does one hear arguments for humans and machines being complements. Uber, for example, has argued that self-driving trucks will increase demand for human drivers and make them more productive.[6] According to Uber, self-driving trucks will pilot the highway miles, while human drivers maneuver the 'last-mile' delivery through complex, urban terrain. This division of tasks will make truck delivery more efficient, driving down prices and increasing demand. In essence, Uber is arguing that self-driving trucks and human drivers are complements, not substitutes.

Both the substitute Chinese labor and the complementary businesses supporting the burgeoning rice trade increasingly undermined the viability of the corvée system. More and more people rejected mandatory conscription and found ways to evade it. To lessen resistance against corvée, the palace gradually reduced the annual length of service from six months to one. The corvée system and its apparatus continued to shrink in the face of the growing market economy.

Realizing that forced labor had no future, the palace gradually dismantled the system. It was officially abolished by King Rama V in 1905. The forces of international trade had, in a span of about 50 years, caused a long dominant sector of the Siamese economy to vanish.

## The Political Aspects of Labor Reform

It is often argued that the abolition of the corvée carried further political significance beyond economic practicality. Specifically, the argument goes, by ending corvée the King was trying to save the country from colonization and improve the image of Siam as a civilized nation in the eyes of the Europeans. This argument carries some weight. Chulalongkorn (Rama V) chose to eliminate slavery – a more limited system of forced labor – around the same time he abolished corvée. By that time, Western powers did not look favorably upon slavery. They also viewed colonization as a way of transforming barbaric nations into civilized people. The ending of forced labor may have contributed to the preservation of Siam's independence.

It is also possible to view the abolition of corvée as an element in Chulalongkorn's grand scheme to centralize administrative power, modernize the country, and avoid colonization. For hundreds of years, the Siamese nobility had posed a challenge to the palace's political dominance because they too enjoyed some control over corvée labor. To wrest power from the aristocrats, Chulalongkorn understood the necessity of depriving them of unlimited access to manpower. By dismantling the corvée system and replacing it with a standing army exclusively under control of the king, political power became fully centralized in Bangkok.

## Nominal and Real Wages

Economists developed the *specific factors model* to explore the effects of international trade. In modern competitive labor markets, economic theory predicts that workers' compensation will equal the marginal productivity of their labor. Hence, most textbook discussions of this model label the vertical axis for diagrams like Figure 3.3 as "wages" instead of "marginal value of labor input." That is why either an increase in the market price of the goods produced by labor or a rise in the capital stock that allows workers to be more productive would serve to increase wages.

Although the model predicts that when foreign demand for rice increases, so do domestic wages, it does not automatically guarantee that trade will increase the *wellbeing* of every laborer. Note that in our model, one of the driving forces behind the rising wages is the increasing price of rice due to foreign demand. If some laborers spend most of their wages on rice and the domestic price of rice increases faster than their wages, then it is possible that their wellbeing will decline as a result of trade. On the other hand, it is also possible that rising wages, together with falling prices for imports, will make many other workers better off.

This consideration of workers' 'wellbeing' points to the important question as to whether wages or the prices of consumer goods are rising faster. Economists distinguish between two types of quantities – nominal and real. If a worker's daily wages have risen from 250 to 300 baht, then we say *nominal wages* have increased by 20%. It is nevertheless important to consider, over the same period of time, what has happened to the prices of goods and services that the worker regularly purchases. If such prices have concomitantly risen by 12%, then we would say the worker's *real wages* have gone up by 8%. Note that it is entirely possible that a worker's real wages have gone down, even though her nominal wages may have gone up.

Returning to nineteenth-century Siam, the fragmented data assembled from historical records has been used by David Feeny[7] to argue that the price of Siam's rice exports rose faster than the drop in the price of cloth imports. Such evidence suggests a rise in the real income of rural workers who grew rice for both consumption and sale. However, urban laborers, who had to purchase rice for their own consumption suffered a decline in real income because their wages did not increase as rapidly as did soaring paddy prices. Although cloth had become more affordable due to imports, it represented a much smaller portion of expenses for the average Siamese at the time.

We again arrive at the familiar conclusion that globalization is not a boon for everyone.

Real and nominal values are also important when discussing interest rates. For example, an 8% nominal interest rate on a loan yields a 5% real interest rate if the annual rate of inflation – the average price increase of all goods and services – is 3%.

## Glossary of Economic Terms

**Opportunity cost**   the opportunity cost of any choice one makes is equal to the sacrifice one must make to pursue that choice.

**Marginal productivity**   the additional output that can be produced by adding an incremental unit of an input. The marginal productivity of labor, for example, is the additional output that can be produced by adding one additional worker or one man-hour (depending on how finely one is allowed to increase).

**Equilibrium**   a state of balance in which forces pushing the outcome in different directions are all equal.

**Substitutes**  products that serve the same purpose/satisfy the same need in the market are called substitute products.

**Complements**  products that are used together and add value to each other are called complementary products.

**Nominal wages**  wages stated without reference to price levels of goods and services in the market.

**Real wages**  wages adjusted for different emerging price levels in the market. For the same nominal wage, the lower the average prices, the higher the real wages.

**Nominal interest rate**  interest rates stated without reference to changes in price levels of goods and services in the market.

**Real interest rate**  interest rates adjusted for how quickly average prices in the market are rising (i.e., adjusted for inflation). For the same nominal interest rate, the higher the real interest rate, the lower the inflation.

## Notes

1 Examples being tea, coffee, sugar, cotton, rubber, indigo and opium.
2 The British also balked when Siam tried to negotiate for similar concessions in trade barriers for her trade with Britain and its colonies.
3 Phongpaichit and Baker, 1995, Table 1.1
4 Irrigation meant cultivation was possible outside of the rainy season, the traditional cultivation period.
5 In the romanticizing of the immigrant Chinese rise from rags to riches, a popular narrative among Thai's is that the patriarchs of today's tycoon families arrived in Siam on a boat with nothing more than *a pillow and a mat*. Their economic success, the story goes, is based on frugality and immense hard work.
6 Madrigal, A. C. (2018, February 1). "Could Self-Driving Trucks Be Good for Truckers?" *The Atlantic.*
7 Feeny, D. (1982). *The Political Economy of Productivity: Thai Agricultural Development, 1880–1975.* University of British Columbia Press. (p. 29)

# Appendix

## Globalization and Its Discontents

The process of Globalization, driven by colonialism, that began in the mid-nineteenth century is often referred to as the 'First Global Economy.' The extent of cross-border integration – the proportion of goods produced in one country and consumed in another – reached its peak just before the First World War (1914–1918). At the peak of the First Global Economy, international finance was governed by the *Gold Standard*. A country's currency was convertible to gold at a fixed rate (e.g., £1 was worth 113 grains of gold while $1 was worth 23.22 grains of gold, where 15.43 grains equaled one gram). An implication of the Gold Standard is that exchange rates are automatically fixed (e.g., £1 was worth 113/23.22 = $4.87) eliminating the risk of exchange rate fluctuations for international traders. The Bowring Treaty of 1855 was negotiated and signed against this backdrop.

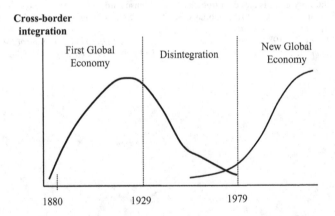

*Figure 3.4* Waves of globalization

The First Global Economy, along with the international financial system regulated by the Gold Standard, wholly collapsed during the interwar years as countries abandoned free trade and mobilized resources to wage war. The New Global Economy that we know today represents the efforts of nations to promote peace and prosperity in the post-war era. This New Global Economy, which gained significant momentum during the last few decades of the twentieth century (Figure 3.4), is governed by international organizations such as the IMF and the WTO. It was during this period that the economies of China and India became increasingly integrated into the world trade system.

One of the major consternations about globalization centers around its purportedly negative impact on domestic workers and their wages. Anti-globalization sentiments regularly center around issues of foreign labor depressing wages of domestic workers. With a minor extension, we can observe such effects in our Specific Factors Model. When there is an influx of foreign workers, the labor pool expands, elongating the horizontal axis of Figure 3.5. Note that the number of workers in both sectors increases, implying that total output has grown. However, the intersection between the marginal productivities of workers in the two sectors slides down lower. What this means is that with the same amount of capital, each additional worker will contribute to greater production, but at a slowing rate. Accordingly, wages fall as the marginal value of labor input in both sectors declines (Figure 3.5).

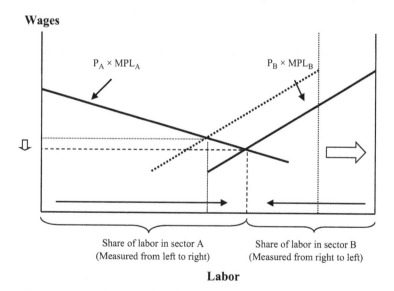

*Figure 3.5* The effect of an enlarged labor pool

Just as we cannot say that a *rise* in nominal wages automatically translates into a rise in workers' wellbeing, so too is it premature to conclude that a *drop* in nominal wages means that the average worker is worse off. Globalization may entail lower prices for many products workers regularly purchase due to greater specialization and competition. When greater purchasing power comes with the same amount of money, real wages get a boost. Recall also that Chinese immigration to Siam in the nineteenth century freed the locals of jobs they did not want to perform, making it possible for them to move to a sector they much more preferred. The welfare consequences of immigration on local workers are thus not immediately ascertained from a unidimensional analysis.

A finer point, and one that the Specific Factors Model is not capable of illustrating, is that not all types of labor are substitutes. While an immigrant can replace a local agricultural laborer, the foreign worker is less likely to be able to compete for jobs as a manager or an agrochemist. In fact, an enlarged pool of agricultural laborers may make the expertise of a farm manager or an agrochemist more valuable. Such might be the case because with an abundance of blue-collar workers, the skills and knowledge of white-collar workers can contribute more to a business's productivity. Hence, while immigrants might be substitutes for some types of domestic workers (making the local blue-collar workers potentially worse off), they might also represent complements to other types of domestic workers (rendering white-collar workers better off), too.

# 4 Production

## Technologies of Paddy Cultivation

*Relevant period*: 1855–1930 (Early Bangkok)
*Economic concepts*: diminishing marginal productivity, isoquant, isocost, marginal rate of technical substitution, cost-minimization

In his international best seller *Outliers*, Malcolm Gladwell[1] proposes an intriguing theory to explain why students from East Asian countries – China, Japan, and South Korea – regularly outperform their peers from other countries in the mathematics section of international standardized exams. Arguing that excelling in mathematics requires dogged persistence, Gladwell theorizes that a common feature among East Asian cultures is the emphasis and exaltation of hard work and perseverance – more so than any other culture. That feature is linked to the rice culture, specifically wet rice cultivation. A culture that extols sacrifice and hard work provides an ideal platform for young people to master mathematics.

To bolster his theory, Gladwell goes on to describe the highly labor-intensive process of wet rice cultivation. According to Gladwell, growing rice in a paddy field is a true feat of engineering. It requires that systems of dykes be painstakingly constructed and a hard clay floor be laid in order to artificially flood the fields. Since rice cannot grow on a solid clay surface, an additional soft bed of mud must be applied before the flooding. At the beginning of the cultivation season, farmers will have an array of seeds to choose from – fast, medium, and slow growing varieties – each containing a different failure risk profile. Crop yield will crucially depend upon the intrinsically unpredictable water supply for the season. In order to prosper, farmers must be adept at calculating contingencies and must also be prepared to handle the risk.

Farmers grow seeds in a nursery for a few weeks before uprooting and transplanting the seedlings – by hand, one at a time – in neat rows in the paddy fields. After this highly labor-intensive process, farmers will continue to monitor the fields to ensure that there is sufficient water to deter weeds but

DOI: 10.4324/9781003392262-4

not so much as to drown the crop. Add to these the tasks of fertilizing, pest control and harvesting, and there is no wonder observers have come to the conclusion that, throughout history, people growing rice have worked harder than any other kind of farmer. The willingness to work hard and make sacrifices for a future reward, according to Gladwell, is ingrained in East Asian culture. Students from this cultural background often appear to have an edge in learning a complicated and demanding subject like mathematics.

Demonstrating whether or not diligence is really an East Asian cultural heritage, and whether such a heritage can translate into superior performance in mathematics is beyond the scope of this chapter. In fact, students from Thailand, another country historically steeped in the culture of wet rice cultivation, do not exhibit remarkable test scores in mathematics, which would seem to at least undercut the universality of the theory. From an economics point of view, however, it is interesting to note that the method of cultivation described by Gladwell, *transplanting*, turns out to be only one among many rice farming techniques. Different rice cultivating 'technologies' have unique advantages and weaknesses. They also require different levels of intensity of inputs – land and labor. As we will see, the choice of an appropriate cultivation technology will depend on the relative abundance of the different production factors.

## Cultivation Technologies

The labor-intensive *transplantation* paradigm described by Gladwell was dominant in the Chao Phraya alluvial plain during the late eighteenth and early nineteenth centuries when rice was grown mainly for subsistence. The limited amount of arable land may have been one reason for the popularity of this labor-intensive technique at that time. The painstaking detail involved in preparing the plot, transplanting the seedlings, and controlling water level, fertilizer and pests helped insure a consistent and predictable harvest. Transplanting, though very labor-intensive, is therefore regarded as a low-risk technology suitable for subsistence cultivation.

There are other cultivation techniques, which require different profiles of input factors, but which also exhibit higher levels of output variation. Under the *broadcasting* scheme, seeds, without a nursery period, are sown directly to a ploughed field. The labor saved from skipping the transplanting process allows farmers to cultivate larger plots of land. The drawback, however, is that the sprouts are distributed unevenly. Broadcast fields therefore tend to receive inferior fertilizing and water control, which leads to a lower yield per unit of land, compared to transplanting. Even so, it is possible for their total output to exceed that of transplanted ones due to the larger sizes of the broadcast plots.

Table 4.1 reports statistics derived from a sample of rice cultivating villages in Southeast Asia. Column (1) gives the average plot size in hectares.

*Table 4.1* Statistics for different paddy cultivation techniques

|  | Average plot size (hectares) | Average yield (tons/hectare) | Yield/plot (tons) | Direct labor required (man-days/ season) |
|---|---|---|---|---|
|  | **(1)** | **(2)** | **(3) = (1) × (2)** | **(4)** |
| **Transplanting** | 2.2 | 2.22 | 4.88 | 292 |
| **Broadcasting** | 4.3 | 1.35 | 5.81 | 179 |

*Source*: Hanks (1972) cited in Feeney (1982).[2]

Broadcasted plots are on average roughly twice the size of transplanted plots (4.3 vs. 2.2 hectares). Despite their smaller average plot size, the direct labor requirement (planting, ploughing, weeding, harvesting, etc.) for transplanted plots reported in column (4) is roughly 63% higher than that of broadcasted plots (292 vs. 179 man-days per season). These data confirm that transplanting represents the more labor-intensive cultivation, while broadcasting is the more land-intensive production technology.

Turning to output, column (2) indicates that transplanting cultivation produces the highest yield per land area – about 2.2 tons per hectare compared to 1.35 tons per hectare generated by broadcasting. This greater productivity per land area of the transplanting method is due to the more even distribution of the seedlings, which results in superior fertilization and pest control. However, when total output is considered in column (3) the broadcasting technique is the more productive (almost 6 tons per plot, compared to less than 5 tons per plot for transplanting), mainly due to the larger average plot size.

Finally, let us calculate the average labor productivity (not reported in Table 4.1) under the two regimes. Using the transplanting method, one person-day of cultivation labor generates about *16.7* kilograms of rice on average (4,880 kilograms/292 person-days). By contrast, one person-day for broadcasting generates on average *32.5* kilograms. The difference here reflects the diminishing marginal productivity of labor. As labor is used more intensively (in the transplanted plots), each additional unit of this input becomes less productive, leading to a lower level of its average productivity.

## Isoquants and the Marginal Rate of Technical Substitution

To better understand the logic behind the choices of different cultivation techniques reported in Table 4.1, let us consider some economic theory of production. Economists like to think that for most types of production, one *input factor* can, to some extent, be substituted for by another. Figure 4.1

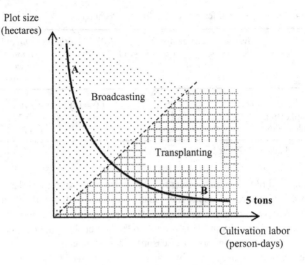

*Figure 4.1* An isoquant showing substitution between land and labor

depicts an *isoquant*, a type of curve, which in this example, represents the different combinations of land and labor that can be used to produce 5 tons of rice. It shows how 5 tons of rice might be produced by 5 farmers working 5 hectares of land, or by 7 farmers working 4 hectares of land. In the latter case, the 2 extra persons put to work monitoring water levels, fertilizing the fields, and controlling pests would improve the yield per acre, resulting in a harvest of 5 tons, even though the amount of paddy land is only 4 hectares.

The isoquant for 4 tons of rice would be to the *southwest* of the ten-ton isoquant, while the isoquant for 6 tons of rice would be toward the *northeast*. The two highlighted regions in Figure 4.1 identify the two types of cultivation regimes earlier discussed. The transplanting technique located to the *south-east* is labor intensive, while the broadcast technique located to the *northwest* is more land intensive.

The slope of the isoquant in Figure 4.1 suggests how substitution is possible between two factors at different levels of abundance. When land is abundant and labor is scarce, the curve is very steep (see point A in the upper left portion of the isoquant in Figure 4.1). This curve indicates that, under such circumstances, large quantities of land could be foregone, while generating the same amount of output, if an extra laborer came on the team. For example, suppose the farmer is cultivating 10 hectares of land, which is more than twice the average plot size for broadcasting. Reducing his plot size by a few hectares would not represent a serious setback to the farming operation. Perhaps, he could manage to generate the *same* output simply by putting in a few more person-days working on a smaller plot.

The opposite is true at the bottom right corner of the curve. When labor is abundant and land is in short supply, we can easily exchange lots of labor for additional land without suffering a decline in output. For example, consider production at point B, where a large family is intensively cultivating a small plot, say 2 hectares. Losing a few workers would not represent a serious setback to such a family's operation, because family members might be getting in each other's way in the crowded field. By expanding the plot size a little, say an acre (roughly a quarter of a hectare), the family could just about make up for the loss in output from less labor input.

The *marginal rate of technical substitution* (MRTS) provides a quantitative measure of the rate of substitution between two factors of production (e.g., land and labor) at a fixed level of output. For instance, at point A sacrificing 2 hectares of land for an additional 30 person-days of weeding could maintain the same level of output, 5 tons. We say, therefore, that the MRTS of *labor for land* at point A is 2 hectares/30 person-days (or 1/15). At point B, on the other hand, an additional acre of land could make up for the loss of 100 person-days of labor. The technical rate of substitution of *labor for land* at point B would therefore be 0.25 hectares/100 person-days (or 1/400). Evidently, the smaller the plot size we begin with, the higher the value of additional land. Likewise, the smaller the size of the workforce we begin with, the higher the value of additional labor. These features of the isoquant are intimately related to the concept of *decreasing marginal productivity* – adding a bit more of an input factor becomes less productive as that factor becomes more abundant. As we will soon see, the MRTS is very important in the process of selecting the most efficient method of production.

## The Isocost and Cost Minimization

Working toward the optimal input combinations a farmer may choose, we introduce a new feature to our diagram, namely the *isocost*. An example shown in Figure 4.2. This one traces the combinations of input factors that would cost the producer the same to acquire. Farm families have limited resources to allocate, either for cultivation or land acquisition. If our hypothetical farm household invested all its resources in acquiring labor for cultivation (through enlisting its own members, hiring from the market etc.), it would be capable of furnishing 900 person-days of labor a year. This maximum labor supply is indicated by the horizontal axis intercept. On the other hand, if every household member were devoted, year-round, to acquiring land, the household would be likely to secure (through renting, clearing forests etc.) *three* acres of land, as indicated by the vertical axis intercept. The line connecting the two intercepts is the isocost. It represents all combinations of labor and land the household can obtain at the same cost.

Clearly, devoting all resources to either cultivation or land acquisition would be foolish, because the household would end up either with no land to

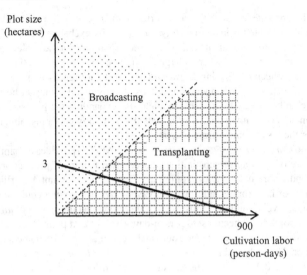

*Figure 4.2* A household's isocost

cultivate or with empty plots. A reasonable allocation of household resources lies between these two extremes. Some resources will be expended to acquire land and some for cultivation. As can be seen in Figure 4.2, the isocost line passes through regions representing both transplanting and broadcasting cultivation. The fairly flat slope drawn here causes most of the line to lie within the transplanting region. If we imagine a steeper slope of that line, it is not difficult to foresee that more of the isocost line would shift toward broadcasting. What makes the slope of the isocost flatter or steeper? If over time, arable land became more abundant, then the household in consideration in Figure 4.2, by expending all its resources acquiring land, would be able to secure *more* than three hectares, and the isocost in Figure 4.2 would be steeper. On the other hand, growing abundance of farm labor would flatten that line.

We are now ready to take our analysis to its logical conclusion. Under these circumstances, what combination of capital and labor would a shrewd farmer select? By combining the isocost and isoquant lines we can find the answer. Consider the three isoquant curves for the output of four, five, and six tons of rice in Figure 4.3. Notice that the four-ton isoquant cuts the isocost line twice. That means that it is possible to produce four tons of rice under some of the combinations of land and labor available to the household. Now consider the six-ton isoquant. This curve lies entirely above the isocost, indicating that *no* combination of the land and labor now available to the household is capable of producing six tons of rice in a year. In other words, producing six tons of paddy would require combinations of land and labor that exceed the present resources of this household.

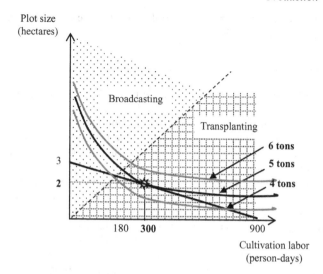

*Figure 4.3* The transplanting method was used for subsistence production

The maximum annual amount of rice they can produce lies somewhere between four and six tons. According to Figure 4.3, the maximum is exactly five tons. We know this because, moving from southwest to northeast, the five-ton isoquant is the highest one touching the isocost line. The point where the five-ton isoquant is tangential to the isocost line pinpoints the optimal allocation of household resources, i.e., two hectares of land and 300 person-days of cultivation labor. As drawn, this relatively labor-intensive production scheme falls within the transplanting regime. We have here an abstract drawing of an optimal production decision which was likely made by a farmer whose family engaged in subsistence agriculture that was prevalent in Siam early in the nineteenth century.

The optimal land-labor combination of two hectares per plot cultivated with roughly 300 person-days of labor per season, as depicted in Figure 4.3, has been drawn to match the numbers reported for the transplanting method in Table 4.1. In fact, up to the mid-nineteenth century, transplanting was commonly used in the areas of the Chao Phraya alluvial plain where there was sufficient and predictable flooding (man-made irrigation systems were minimal at this time in Siam). Land suitable for cultivation was limited, and rice was mainly grown for consumption within the household. To avoid the potential catastrophe of starvation from a poor yield, it made sense for households to direct virtually all of their resources toward cultivating the family's small plot of land. Under these circumstances, employing the transplanting method was the natural choice. However, when trade with the West intensified in the mid-nineteenth century, booming markets for agricultural products promoted the development and acceptance by farmers of new cultivation techniques.

## The Canal Projects

Siam's rice exports accelerated during the mid-nineteenth century, boosted by the signing of the Bowring treaty with Britain in 1855. Beginning in the 1870s, growing world demand, together with falling freight rates combined to produce a boom in the world market. From the 1860s to the 1930s, Siam's rice exports grew at an astounding rate from around 100,000 tons per year to 1.5 million tons per year.[3]

Booming demand, coupled with a labor force expanded by large numbers of war slaves and immigrants, drove the Siamese elite to invest in opening up the amount of land under cultivation in the Central Plain. This was accomplished by numerous canal-digging projects aimed at draining the extensive marshlands surrounding Bangkok. The most famous of these projects was the scheme to drain six hundred thousand acres of land in the Rangsit area north of Bangkok. Financed by the palace and a host of aristocratic families, the Rangsit canal project turned out to be a success. Land prime for cultivation along the canals was meted out in large tracks to project shareholders. The elite then became lords of the land, deriving income from the peasant rice farmers who were their tenants.

As a result of the sudden expansion of paddy land and the rising demand for rice exports, transplanting began to be replaced by broadcasting, which emerged as the more advantageous method of cultivation. The increasing abundance of desirable land following the canal projects of the mid-to-late nineteenth century is depicted in Figure 4.4 by a clockwise rotation of the isocost line. The rising supply of land made the acquisition of this resource less costly. A greater portion of the isocost line now passes through the broadcasting region. With more land available, each household became better able to grow and harvest more rice. According to Figure 4.4, the new maximum output, given the adjusted isocost line, is six tons of rice. Crucially, the land-labor combination at the optimal output – 4 hectares and 180 person-hours per season – falls inside the broadcasting region. With this new production regime, fewer resources are devoted to cultivation and more to the acquisition of farm land. The optimal input combination is drawn to reflect the estimates reported in Table 4.1.

Are theoretical predictions born out in the data? Siam's total rice output did indeed significantly increase after the canal projects made irrigation easier and more dependable. Moreover, records show that by 1930, broadcasted rice accounted for about 70% of paddy output in the Central Plain.[4] Our economic model does a respectable job in reasoning out what historical records confirm.

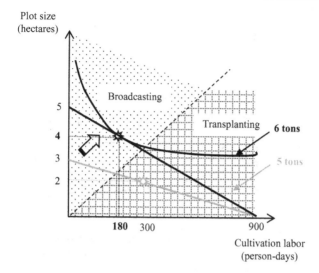

*Figure 4.4* The switch to broadcasting cultivation

## The Return of Transplanting

As irrigated land gradually became fully occupied, the transplant regime staged a comeback. The population grew and labor once again became the relatively more abundant input factor. By the early 1960s, roughly 60% of Central Plain paddy production was taking place via the transplant method of cultivation.[5]

Graphically, one can conceptualize the switch back to transplanting as a counter-clockwise rotation of the isocost line. Figure 4.5 illustrates such a shift. A greater portion of the isocost now lies within the transplanting area. The maximum output under the rotated isocost is 5 tons per plot, produced by two hectares of land and 300 person-hours of cultivation. Production technology switched back to transplanting.

At this point, you may wonder how much of this optimization model of paddy production is grounded in reality. The model does a good job at explaining the pattern of the changing rice production schemes – from transplanting to broadcasting and then back to transplanting again – over our period of interest. It also offers a coherent logic, linking changes in the external environment to the evolving choices of the producers. Nonetheless, one could still ask if nineteenth- and twentieth-century Siamese peasants in fact made optimal decisions by choosing the most advantageous combinations of input factors such as land and labor.

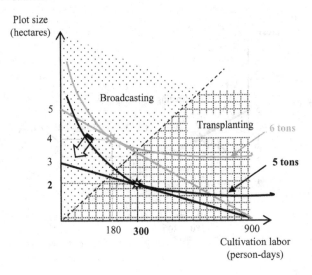

*Figure 4.5* The return of transplanting cultivation

To answer this perceptive question, let us begin by presuming that farmers, like everyone else, make a variety of decisions, the results of which some are pleasing and some are disappointing. When a farmer's choices are suitable to the prevailing environment, they support a competitive edge. When a farmer does well, he can support a larger family. Farmers who make uninformed or unwise choices face the opposite. Successful choices, especially those determining livelihood, are often copied and many even become standard. Under these reasonable assumptions, one can see how an optimal production scheme would quickly spread, even becoming the norm throughout society. Using this simple and intuitive evolutionary logic, we can see that our model of optimized production makes a good deal of sense.

## Slash-and-Burn: A Third Cultivation Technique

As every square inch of the Chao Phraya alluvial plain was being transformed into paddy fields, peasants began to feel pressure to seek out arable land beyond the Central Plain. More and more settlements appeared in the northern uplands and the northeastern plateau. Methods for cultivating rice along these new frontiers were brutal. The geography of the frontier – mainly forests – promoted a third rice cultivating technique, namely *slash-and-burn*.

Under slash-and-burn, also referred to as *shifting* cultivation, farmers clear plots of forest land and set fire to any remaining vegetation. The ash left over would serves as fertilizer for the new fields. Seeds are planted in the un-ploughed soil with the help of a dibble stick. The growers relied on the thin but fertile soil of the newly cleared land to produce a successful crop. The lack of irrigation, however, meant that output could be highly variable, depending on the amount of precipitation. Typically, the quality top soil on the slopes of the denuded hills was soon washed away by the annual rains, further destabilizing the hillside environment. After a few years, such soil could no longer support crops. Farmers would then seek out and shift to a new area. Slash and burn communities often moved every few years in search of fertile areas. The impact of such nomadic practices would cause significant deforestation, the long-term costs of which have never been properly considered.

Table 4.2 reproduces the numbers from Table 4.1, with the addition of statistics for slash-and-burn, the average plot size for which is by far the smallest, at 1.5 hectares per plot. Although the plot size is relatively small, the actual land requirement for this technique is much larger. These nomads eventually abandon old plots for new ones when the richness of forest top soil is depleted. Slash-and-burn agriculture appears to be relatively labor intensive at 255 person-days per season. Most of the labor is used to clear new plots of land. These dry rice farmers do *not* build dikes, plough fields, monitor water levels, apply fertilizers, and eliminate pests as transplanting cultivators do.

The average yield of a slash-and-burn plot is rather low, at 1.47 tons per hectare, a number comparable to the average yield per hectare of a broadcasted plot. When yield per plot is considered, slash-and-burn cultivation comes in the lowest at 2.21 tons per plot, due both to the small plot size and to the low yield per hectare. Average labor productivity (not reported in Table 4.2) is also the lowest for the slash-and-burn scheme – *9* kilograms per person-day (2,210 kilograms/255 person days) compared to that of broadcasting (*19* kilograms per person-day) and transplanting (*11* kilograms per person-day) cultivation.

*Table 4.2* Slash-and-burn cultivation compared to other techniques

| | Average plot size (hectares) | Average yield (tons/hectare) | Yield/plot (tons) | Labor requirements (man-days/ season) |
|---|---|---|---|---|
| | **(1)** | **(2)** | **(3) = (1) × (2)** | **(4)** |
| **Transplanting** | 2.2 | 2.22 | 4.88 | 292 |
| **Broadcasting** | 4.3 | 1.35 | 5.81 | 179 |
| **Slash-and-burn** | 1.5 | 1.47 | 2.21 | 255 |

*Source:* Hanks (1972) cited in Feeney (1982).

## Isoquants and Isocosts – Further Remarks

The geometric analyses involving isoquants and isocost curves illustrated in Figures 4.1 through 4.4 are standard in the field of microeconomics. According to standard lingo, firms make their production decisions based on the principle of cost-minimization. The principle goes something like this. The firm decides on a quantity of output it wants to produce. This amount of output can be manufactured using the various combinations of input factors depicted by an isoquant curve. What combination does the firm choose? The answer is likely to be the one that requires the minimum cost, represented by the point of tangency where the lowest isocost curve just touches the selected isoquant.

In modern markets where production input factors have clearly defined "prices," the slope of the isocost carries a particularly important interpretation. Going back to our example in Figure 4.3, as the supply of land becomes more abundant, an economist would expect its price (i.e., rent) to fall. The fall in rent will make the slope of the isocost steeper, resulting in a new cost-minimizing production scheme that is more land-intensive than before (i.e., the broadcast method). When labor becomes more abundant and wages decline, the opposite would happen. There would be a switch back toward labor-intensive transplanting such as occurred in the Chao Phraya Central Plains by the mid-twentieth century.

Readers who remember their high school algebra will recognize that the slope of the *isocost* mathematically corresponds to the ratio of the prices of the factor inputs. In our example, the slope represents the ratio of wages (the price of labor) to rent (the price of land). The slope of the *isoquant* – also known as the MRTS – at the point of tangency with the isocost (the cost minimizing scheme) must also be equal to the ratio of input prices. Put succinctly, in the cost minimizing production scheme:

$$MRTS_{labor \ for \ land} = \frac{Price \ of \ labor \ (wages)}{Price \ of \ land \ (rent)}$$

Here, *wages* would be measured in baht per day while *rent* would be measured in *baht per hectare per cultivation season*.

To develop some intuition about the equation above, let's consider what would happen if the equation did not balance. Suppose the MRTS (the left-hand side) is smaller than the ratio of prices (the right-hand side). This would suggest that giving up 1 man-day of labor (and enjoy savings on the wage) would need to be compensated for by a quantity of land smaller than $\frac{wage}{rent}$ hectares. How much would such land cost? It would cost*less* than a day's wage. Therefore, cutting back on labor and expanding the cultivation area would result in more output. A smart farmer would figure this out sooner or later and rearrange his production accordingly.

What if the MRTS were larger than the ratio of prices. Using similar logic as that outlined above, we can conclude that the farmer could increase his output by cutting back on some land use and increasing labor input. Again, we would expect someone, sooner or later, to discover such a rearrangement and exploit it. The only arrangement that cannot be improved upon by tinkering with the land/labor ratio is the one that satisfies the above equation. Such an arrangement is an equilibrium, a state that once reached will exhibit stability.

## Epilogue: From Land to Robots

The focus of this chapter has been on agricultural production, a sector that used to represent a dominant share of the Thai economy, but today accounts for only about a tenth of the Kingdom's total production. In many developing economies, the manufacturing sector is gradually over taking the dominance of agriculture. Beginning in the 1960s Thailand, for example, focused on its domestic light industries, including textiles, footwear, and jewelry. These light industries were gradually replaced by increasingly more advanced production such as automobiles, electronics and computer parts.

The initial jump from an agrarian-based economy to one supported by light industries is often predicated on the availability of abundant, cheap labor. From the East Asian Tigers[6] of the 1970s, to Thailand in the 1980s, and to Vietnam, Cambodia, and Bangladesh in the 2000s, the labor-intensive garment sector has proven to be a reliable gateway to industrialization.

While the East Asian Tigers have fully industrialized, other developing Asian economies appear to be facing challenges that earlier Tigers did not encounter. *First*, the spread of birth control and the entry of women into the labor force have greatly reduced the population growth rates of developing economies around the world. Countries such as China and Thailand are projected to enter the early stages of 'aging society' in the coming decades, most likely before achieving high-income status. *Second*, rapid improvement in mechatronics has increased the use of robotic labor. Machines are now poised to take over many human jobs, especially the simpler and more repetitive ones. The busy, noisy factories of the past are being hushed as robots replace human workers and outdated technology.

Adopting the model we developed in this chapter, let us assume a garment factory is faced with a (simplified) choice of selecting a combination of two factors of production – human labor and robots. What does the model predict for the future of work in the manufacturing sector? A declining birth rate suggests a shrinking labor supply, and hence a steeper isocost as drawn in Figure 4.6. Progress in mechatronics, making robots cheaper and more reliable, contributes to two separate developments. First, it further steepens the isocost curve by making robots more affordable. Second, it *flattens* the isoquant curve in Figure 4.6 by *reducing* the MRTS, in other words reducing the rate at which human workers are substituted for by robots. For instance, a robot may have replaced 5 human workers (0.2 robots/worker) in the past, but, due to their increased agility and intelligence, might now be able to replace 20 human workers (0.05 robots/worker).

Figure 4.6 illustrates a cost minimization scheme in which *all* human labor is replaced with robots. In mathematical jargon, such a situation is referred to as a *corner solution* – a condition under which circumstances are so stacked against humans that a cost-minimizing factory is no longer willing to use them as robot-replacements. To be clear, the model does not predict that such an extreme conclusion will come to pass. However, it represents the limit case for when robots become more and more efficient in completing manufacturing tasks and the human labor pool gradually ages and shrinks.

It is important to remember that we began this discussion focusing on manufacturing jobs. Even if all manufacturing jobs were turned over to robots, other types of work, would likely require a human touch, for example, teaching yoga or being a physical therapist. Service sector jobs have disadvantages when it comes to boosting a country's average income. First, the number of such jobs are presently quite small, compared to mass employment in factories. Second, unlike textiles and electronic components, service sector jobs are difficult to export. The growth of a country's service sector is usually limited to the size of its domestic market (plus perhaps foreign tourists). Developmental economists are therefore skeptical about the prospects of sustained economic growth led by the service sector.

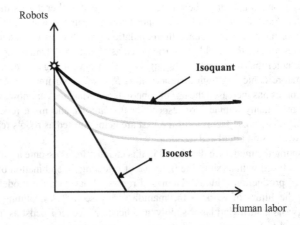

*Figure 4.6* A factory choosing between robots and human labor

However, as there are increasing population shifts and migration due to climate change and other social upheavals, new arrivals represent new resources and bring knowledge and skills which have transformative potential for the hosting economy. For example, incoming refugees bring new knowledge and market possibilities in areas of food preparation, life-style, human services, and the arts. Such transformations, if accepted and appreciated, may represent an additional ray of hope.

The point of the discussion in this section is not to paint a dystopian picture of future competition between humans and robots. The intention is to illustrate that the key concepts and ideas introduced in the chapter are relevant not only for analyzing the decisions of Siamese paddy farmers in the late nineteenth century but are also pertinent for understanding the future of global societies and manufacturing.

## Glossary of Economic Terms

**Diminishing marginal productivity**  the *diminishing* additional output that can be produced by adding an incremental unit of an input. For example, adding a tenth worker to the work on a paddy field will lead to a smaller incremental increase in output compared to that contributed by the fifth worker.

**Isoquant**  a graph showing all the combinations of input factors (e.g., land and labor) that can be used to produce the same quantity of output (e.g., paddy).

**Isocost**  a graph showing all the combinations of input factors (e.g., land and labor) that can be acquired at the same total cost.

**Marginal rate of technical substitution**  the rate at which an increase in one input factor (e.g., labor) can compensate for the reduction in another input factor (e.g., land) in such a way that the total output (e.g., paddy) does not change.

**Cost-minimization**  the process of identifying the lowest total cost of acquiring all necessary inputs to produce a pre-specified amount of output.

## Notes

1 Gladwell, M. (2011). *Rice Paddies and Math Tests, in Outliers: The Story of Success*. Back Bay Books.
2 Feeney, D. (1982). *The Political Economy of Productivity: Thai Agricultural Development, 1880–1975*. University of British Columbia Press, Vancouver, Canada.
3 Phongpaichit and Baker (1995, table 1.1).
4 Indra Montri (1930) cited in Feeney (1982).
5 Behrman (1968) cited in Feeney (1982).
6 The East Asian Tiger economies refer to South Korea, Taiwan, Hong Kong and Singapore.

# 5　Institutions
## Rent Seeking and Clientelism

*Relevant period:* 1951–1980 (the Cold War era)
*Economic concepts:* Gross Domestic Product, economic growth, institutions, clientelism, financial intermediation, upgrading

When the reign of Chulalongkorn (Rama V) came to an end at the beginning of the twentieth century, the Siamese economy entered a period of decline. Two World Wars and the Great Depression were about to wreak havoc in peoples' lives, hamper trade, and limit economic opportunity. The European shipping, trading and banking businesses that had bloomed in Siam during the *First Global Economy* (1880–1929) would be forced to depart, leaving behind a vacuum that turned into major post-war commercial opportunities for alert entrepreneurs. The overseas Chinese community in Siam were well poised to take advantage of these openings.

The business community also had to contend with radical changes in the political environment. The Communist Revolution in China forced the local over-seas Chinese community to sever ties with the mainland and commit its future to their adopted homeland. Thailand's 1932 revolution had overturned the absolute power of the monarchy, gradually transferring political power into the hands of the military. Commercial success in Thailand would no longer depend directly on palace connections, but now required the backing of the military top brass.

Beginning in the early 1960s, the economic influence of the United States in Thailand intensified significantly. The Vietnam war brought US military personnel to the beaches of Pattaya for rest and recoperation, jump starting the tourism industry that would flourish in the following decades. Fear of the spread of communist ideology spurred a flow of unprecedented military and development aid into Thailand, a staunch ally of America in the Cold War. Between 1951 and 1975, two and a half billion dollars in US military aid and over six hundred million dollars in non-military financial assistance were

DOI: 10.4324/9781003392262-5

poured into Thailand. Additional World Bank loans of close to half a billion dollars for infrastructure development such as highways, dams, and schools stoked a spending and investment frenzy.

Despite the unprecedented influx of foreign capital, this investment did not swamp the local economy. Most investment was still homebased. However, a boom sparked in part by foreign aid resulted in strong and sustained economic performance in Thailand over several decades. While economists today continue to debate the effectiveness of foreign aid as a development tool, American economic assistance to Thailand during the Cold War era has a strong claim to being one of the success stories. An important factor contributing to this success was local entrepreneurial energy. The overseas Chinese community were major players in key investments driving economic growth throughout this period. In this chapter, we will explore how the local Chinese business community adapted to the new economic environment, skillfully taking advantage of the spate of opportunities, greatly expanding their role as one of the main forces driving the economic success of Thailand during the mid-twentieth century.

## The King of Textiles

*"I have become the man I am today because of my army connections,"* Sukree Photiratanagkun, one of Thailand's legendary textile tycoons, is known to have proclaimed. From the end of World War II through Thailand's big industrialization push in the 1960s, the prosperity of overseas Chinese merchants hinged primarily on their ability to access and use their military patron's influence to cut business deals.

Sukree, a first-generation Chinese immigrant from Hainan, was a master of political opportunism. In 1949, while still a budding textile entrepreneur, he managed to obtain from Prime Minister Phibun a contract to exclusively supply uniforms for the army. When Phibun was ousted by a coup in 1957, Sukree somehow secured the favor of Sarit, Thailand's new strongman, and took over the army's spinning mills at Wat Soi Thong, further expanding his production capacity.

Between 1984 and 1987, domestic yarn prices shot up by more than 50%. Sukree's factory, by then the dominant local producer, came under scrutiny for illegal price manipulation. The allegations looked certain to derail Sukree's application for the crucial government support he needed for his planned capacity expansion. Such a disruption would be a disastrous blow, gifting a big break to his arch rival, a textile group under the patronage of General Pramarn. In a stunning turn of events, however, the Minister of Industry visited Sukree's production facility, declared the factory's operations satisfactory, and confirmed the government's support for Sukree's expansion. It was later rumored that the advantageous turn of events was engineered by

Colonel Chareonsak, a well-connected, ex-intelligence officer who was none other than Sukree's son-in-law.

## How a Country Grows Rich

Beginning in the mid-twentieth century, the economy of Thailand grew at a pace unprecedented in its history. As the economy branched out from one based primarily on agriculture to one based on a more diversified portfolio of agribusiness, manufacturing, and services, the average income of Thai citizens increased significantly.

Stories of wheeling and dealing such as those involving the textile tycoon Sukree make for stimulating business case studies. Yet, the accounts remind us of corrupt politicians and crony businessmen common in some of the poorest countries in the world today. For an economy in the midst of modernization such as Thailand during the second half of the twentieth century, why did such plagues not completely derail economic development?

### *A Short Detour on How Economic Progress Is Measured*

At the most basic level, macroeconomists measure economic development using a concept called Gross Domestic Product (GDP) per capita. First, let us clarify what GDP means. GDP is *the total market value of all finished goods and services produced in a country in a year*. Intuitively, this quantity is the sum of the market prices of all new domestic production bought and sold during the year. The term 'finished' is added to avoid double counting the value of intermediate goods, once as an input (e.g., the value of the eggs the baker buys as ingredients for his cake) and again as part of the final product (e.g., the value of the cake the baker sells to his customers). The term 'domestic' emphasizes that GDP does not include foreign production. Finally, it is important to note that GDP only counts new production, not the stock of merchandise produced in past years.

GDP 'per capita' refers to GDP divided by the country's population. It measures the value of goods and services each person in a country would command if all of a country's output were equally shared among its citizens. In 1951, Thailand was an agrarian economy, largely based on paddy cultivation. Economists figure that GDP per capita in 1951 was equivalent in the *year-2005* to a purchasing power of US$938 (Figure 5.1). Note that GDP numbers are conventionally converted to US dollars for cross-country comparisons. The "year-2005" part specifies a point in time to imagine the purchasing power of US$938, given the fact that rising prices (inflation) gradually erodes the purchasing power of US$1.

The World Bank's international poverty line was US$1.25 per day in 2005 and rose to US$1.90 in 2011. By international standards, we can therefore take

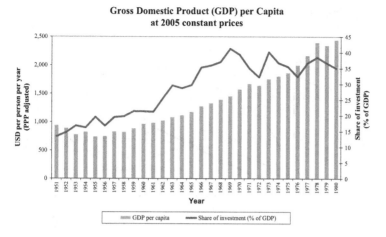

*Figure 5.1* GDP per capita and investment share, 1951–1980

the poverty line to be somewhere between US$450 and US$700 per person per year. Given a per capita GDP of US$938, the average Thai person in 1951 lived above poverty, but not by much. Fast forward 30 years, the GDP per capita in Thailand had grown by more than two and a half times to US$2,442, placing the country firmly in the middle-income category. Such progress is not to be taken lightly because it does not happen everywhere. For example, in 1951 Kenya and Nigeria were both slightly richer than Thailand. Their average incomes per capita were slightly above a thousand dollars per person per year. However, those two nations did not achieve persistent economic growth over the ensuing three decades. By 1980, Thailand was, by comparison, more than twice as prosperous.

How can we explain such a consequential phenomenon?

## The Solow Growth Model

Economic growth is fundamentally a cumulative process. Present consumption must be foregone for the potential of achieving increased output in the future. This process of present sacrifice for future affluence is known in economics as saving and investment. Citizens must jointly determine what portion of the country's total output (GDP) they want allocated to current consumption such as spending on appliances and festivities and what portion to savings for investment in future growth. The *Solow model* formalizes these ideas.

According to Figure 5.2, a country's output per capita (GDP per capita) is determined by a production function, *f(k)*, where the argument *k* represents society's capital stock per worker. The long-run or 'steady-state' level of

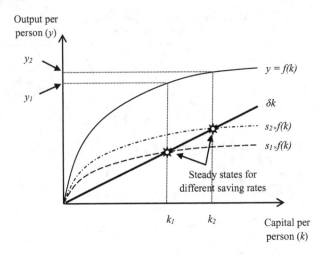

*Figure 5.2* Output growth according to the Solow model

output is determined by the interaction between two quantities – investment and depreciation. In the long run, investment equals the portion of output saved, denoted in the figure as $s \times f(k)$ where $s$ is the rate of saving. By assuming that capital depreciates at a constant rate, $\delta$, depreciation is simply an upward-sloping, straight line in Figure 5.2. Whenever investment exceeds depreciation, the capital stock per worker grows. Similarly, whenever depreciation exceeds investment, the capital stock per worker declines. This logic leads to the conclusion that an economy's output per worker should gradually move toward the point where investment equals depreciation, the *steady state* level of output in the long run.

Figure 5.2 depicts two economies with similar rates of depreciation but different rates of saving. The economy with the higher saving rate ($s_2$) invests more and converges toward a higher level of per capita capital ($k_2$) and output ($y_2$).

The Solow model predicts that economic growth in the long run is correlated with higher levels of savings and investment. Figure 5.1 shows that growth in output in Thailand was accompanied by a significant increase in investment. In 1951, the country's average share of investment as a percent of GDP was around 15%. This share doubled to 30% by the mid-1960s and remained above that level through 1980. Figure 5.2 also implies that countries with higher levels of savings (and thus higher investments) will grow toward steady-states with higher levels of output per capita than countries with lower levels of investment. While Thailand was allocating close to one third of its output to investment during the 1960s and 1970s, the investment ratios in Kenya and Nigeria were about 17% and 6%, respectively. This disparity, which of course also reflects the particular social and political obstacles burdening these two countries, likely explains the difference in economic performance between Thailand and these two African nations.

## Why Do Some Countries Invest More Than Others?

As the experiences of numerous under-developed economies around the world show, ensuring sufficient investment for future economic prosperity is not something that happens automatically. Economists identify *risk* as a major deterrent to saving and investment. Putting stock in the future is inherently a risky endeavor. After weighing the risks involved, potential entrepreneurs in many societies simply decide that investing is not a worthwhile activity. When such is the case, economic growth is stalled. What are some of the major risks we are talking about here?

Most fundamentally, the investor risks not surviving long enough to enjoy the fruits of his investment. Wars or other forms of political violence can very effectively destroy incentives to save and invest.

A second important risk of investment is arbitrary confiscation of the invested capital or output. Autocratic governments often 'nationalize' private enterprises whenever there is concern over government instability or when there is a regime change. Nationalization is often done in the name of justice or social good although the true benefactors are invariably the dictator and his cronies. Such arbitrary confiscation not only discourages domestic investment but also scares away potential foreign investors, suppliers of capital and essential technologies.

Macroeconomic mismanagement represents a third source of investment risk. Governments in developing economies often cannot resist the temptation of resorting to printing money to finance their various fiscal needs. An enlarged monetary base inevitably leads to high inflation. According to a maxim in macroeconomics, high inflation is synonymous with variable inflation. When creditors cannot make reasonable predictions about the value of money over time, they reduce their amount of lending, thus thwarting new investment. High inflation coupled with draconian price controls reduces investment even further. Who in their right mind would put in the effort to produce valuable goods and services in exchange for a few worthless pieces of paper?

Finally, a tolerable level of risk is sometimes not sufficient to ensure investment. Government- protected monopolies often have little incentive to absorb new technologies, increase efficiency, or reduce prices. In economies that harbor large, protected monopolies, a few oligarchs enjoy incredible profits as they run inefficient enterprises at the expense of domestic consumers. To encourage efficiency enhancing investments, therefore, some pressure in the form of market competition is usually required. It is no wonder that the most efficient and innovative corporations today operate in intensely competitive markets.

## Managing Investment Risk the Traditional Way: Institutions

Advanced economies use institutional arrangements to manage the risk inherent in investing for the future. *Institutions*, a concept borrowed from sociology, are man-made structures of rules and norms that shape expectations of individual behavior and group interactions. Institutions, supported by laws, regulation and social conventions, are long-lived and slow to change. While family, religion, mass media, art, and culture are all examples of important social institutions, the institutions that are principally involved in managing investment risk are a society's *political, economic,* and *legal* systems.

Successful countries possess *political systems* that can manage conflict and reliably safeguard a peaceful transference of political power. Stable democracies, for example, settle disagreement through majority rule and manage the transition from one political leader to another through a combination of widely accepted laws and tradition. Once in power, leaders of the government routinely ensure that the basic functions of the state, including maintaining national defense and upholding cordial relationships with neighboring countries, are properly discharged. The administration of such functions in healthy democracies is done in a predictable manner that discourages corruption, cronyism, or abuse of power.

Strong *economic and legal institutions* uphold, support, and regulate private property rights and markets. Arbitrary confiscation of property is prohibited, both on paper and in practice. When disputes arise over property rights, courts reliably adjudicate matters in a timely and predictable manner, and such legal decisions are viewed as fair and evenhanded by most members of the community. Regulators do their best to promote fair competition in the marketplace, and remain vigilant against the abuse of market power by dominant, incumbent businesses. Finally, macroeconomic policy is entrusted in the hands of capable administrators, who judiciously control the supply of money to maintain price stability, and keep at bay potential devastation from rampant inflation.

High-quality institutions no doubt play an essential role in the process by which countries grow rich. In fact, we often observe that it is the rich countries that possess the highest-quality institutions. Returning to our story about Thailand in the mid-twentieth century, we immediately notice significant shortfalls in the country's institutional performance. We hear stories about military coup d'états and strongmen seizing political power through force. The account of Sukree and his army patrons is fraught with corruption and cronyism. Favorable treatment is meted out based on personal connection, not through merit or fair competition. Finally, the courts and regulators have remained entirely absent from their presumed roles of promoting fair competition and upholding the rule of law.

Given such shortcomings, it is surprising that between 1951 and 1980, Thailand's GDP per capita grew by about 160%. Investment also climbed from 15% to 35% of GDP. Even the country's institutional weaknesses did not create high enough investment risks to completely stunt economic growth. In the next section, we will introduce a framework to explain how Thailand, despite its poor-quality institutions, managed to invest and record strong economic growth during this period.

## Capital Accumulation and Growth-Facilitating Institutions in Thailand

Having identified the basic prerequisites for economic growth, we now consider the institutional arrangements in Thailand that helped keep investment risk within tolerable bounds, while at the same time, ensuring enough competitive pressure to facilitate the modernization of the Thai economy during the second half of the twentieth century.

After the 1932 revolution that overthrew the absolute monarchy, the political environment in Thailand quickly gravitated toward military dictatorship. Initially, the official policy of the military-led regime was to nationalize industries and empower rural peasants by limiting the role of local ethnic Thai-Chinese capitalists. While numerous state-owned enterprises were set up in the 1930s and 1940s to deal with all kinds of businesses from rice trading to retail and distribution, certain civilian-led factions of the regime managed to implement policies that ran counter to the official blueprint.

Pridi Bhanomyong, the leader of the contrarians, was a marginalized civilian leader of the 1932 revolution. He initially championed nationalization, but later had a change of heart after witnessing faltering state-owned businesses. Pridi grew to prefer joint ventures between the state and local Thai-Chinese businessmen over bureaucrat-managed enterprises. While the performances of state-owned enterprises were less than spectacular, private joint ventures in banking, insurance, trading, and construction prospered. The success of Pridi and his associates was significant. It served as a potent example for subsequent political leaders. By showing greater appreciation for the contribution of the private sector, Pridi demonstrated that harnessing the power of capital could create greater surplus for all parties involved.

Bolstered by American Cold War ideology and foreign aid, the military tightened its grip on politics in the 1950s and 1960s. For practical reasons, both domestic (the bad experience with state enterprises) and foreign (the anti-communism ideology), the generals encouraged participation from the private sector in driving the economy forward. While investment and operational decisions were entrusted to civilian entrepreneurs, mostly Sino-Thai businessmen, the generals played the role of 'patrons', guaranteeing security from harassment and stable access to resources and markets. Such an arrangement, known as 'clientelism,' was mutually beneficial for all parties involved. The generals received handsome payoffs to supplement their modest government salaries, while the businessmen enjoyed de facto protection of their property – a crucial benefit that would not at that time have been guaranteed by Thailand's rudimentary legal and economic institutions.

A key to the relative success of the clientelism model in Thailand was that patrons were powerful enough to guarantee protection but not so powerful as to be able to eliminate all competition for their clients. While property rights were sufficiently protected, competition was not thwarted.

Doner and Ramsay (2000)[1] offer a fascinating account of the development of the Thai textile industry in the 1950s and 1960s. They point to incidents where incumbent manufacturers under the protection of highly influential political figures failed to block new entries into the market because of the fractional nature of government. Regardless of the identities of the incumbents, new entrepreneurs could always find a patron among politicians, generals, or senior bureaucrats powerful enough to facilitate their market entry. The overlapping responsibilities of different organizations within the government bureaucracy made anti-competitive policies virtually impossible to implement effectively.

> At least four agencies – the Board of Investment, and the commerce, industry, and finance ministries – controlled trade policy. Five departments in three ministries influenced access to permits and licenses. Politically, this pattern of policy-making allowed patrons in a range of agencies to satisfy particular groups of supporters. Economically, it meant that the Thai state was strikingly incapable of imposing capacity controls.
>
> (Doner and Ramsay, 2000, p. 159)

Such a lack of coordination led to severe competitive pressure for textile manufacturers. Attempts to softened competition by entry limits and capacity controls regularly faltered.

> In 1974, for example, the government banned new plants and expansion of capacity in spinning, but the number of spindles climbed from 1,094,000 in 1975 to approximately 1,600,000 by the end of 1982. In the mid-1980s, these unregistered mills accounted for an estimated 30 percent of production. ... One of the most spectacular cases of lack of co-operation among state officials occurred in 1983, when Sukree Photiratanagkun's Thai Melon Textiles received permission from the Ministry of Industry to install 125,440 spindles and 1,000 looms, but actually installed an extra 44,800

spindles and 358 looms above the allowed numbers. The Department of Textiles in the Ministry of Industry discovered the violation, ordered him to disassemble the additional machines and threatened him with a jail sentence. Sukree approached Prime Minister Prem Tinsulanond for help, met with army commander General Arthit Kamlang-ek, and petitioned the Board of Investment to allow him to keep the extra machines. The case was finally settled in the Ministry of Industry's Textile Policy Committee. The committee allowed him to continue operating the spindles and looms, with the stipulation that he had to establish a bonded warehouse which would use the production of the additional equipment only for exports.

(Doner and Ramsay, 2000, pp. 159–160)

The final ingredient facilitating investment and economic growth was Thailand's exemplary management of a stable macroeconomic environment in the mid-twentieth century. Perhaps due to incredible luck, the Bank of Thailand, the country's monetary authority, developed a strong reputation of integrity and technocratic competence during the 50s and 60s. The prestige and respect the central bank enjoyed allowed it to negotiate a significant amount of autonomy from political influence. By keeping a tight control over money supply, the Thai economy benefited from low inflation during the early years of its industrialization. As discussed earlier, price stability represents an important prerequisite for saving and investment.

An indirect benefit from the stable monetary policy was that it naturally constituted a 'hard budget constraint' for the government. When a government cannot resort to printing money to finance its various expenses, it faces restrictions on its ability to bail out failing businesses. Thus, businesses in Thailand during the period under consideration were presented with a sensible set of incentives – operate efficiently and keep your profits as rewards, but do not depend on being saved by your government connections if you cannot survive the competition.

To summarize, competitive clientelism facilitated adequate protection of property rights to ensure that investments were forthcoming, while at the same time allowing competitive pressure to stimulate businesses to cut cost and improve efficiency. A stable macroeconomic environment assured businesses that their investments were safe, but also that government bailouts would not materialize if they failed to achieve competitiveness.

## Financial Intermediation: The Commercial Banks

So far, we have assumed that turning savings into investments happens automatically. Such an assumption is unrealistic. In practice, an intermediary that links savers and borrowers is often required. Commercial banks traditionally fulfill this intermediary role. They aggregate savings from a broad range of depositors, scan the business landscape for promising investments, disburse loans, monitor borrowers, and collect and pay interest at competitive rates – doing all of this while ensuring that the risk of default remains acceptable and that sufficient reserves are available in case depositors wish to withdraw their funds.

A well-operating banking sector, traditionally the backbone of an economy's financial system, is critical for investing and for sustained economic growth. Yet, maintaining a well-functioning commercial banking system is not straightforward. Banks need to retain the trust of their depositors, to invest conservatively, and to remain solvent in times of economic downturn. In advanced economies, a stable banking industry is achieved through a combination of a history of credibility and trust, effective laws, and capable and trustworthy regulators such as a central bank.

The commercial banks that mobilized savings and investments in Thailand during the 1960s were organized around Thai-Chinese business families. The so-called *"Big Four Families"* that controlled the four major commercial banks and their sprawling, conglomerate-like business interest were:

Sophonpanit family (Bangkok Bank)
Lamsam family (Thai Farmers Bank)
Techaphaibun family (Bangkok Metropolitan Bank)
Rattanarak family (Bank of Ayudhya)

Each of these family-controlled banks mobilized funds from domestic savings to finance investments in a variety of businesses, including agro-industries, trading and exporting, textiles, construction, transportation, liquor, and insurance. They all maintained strong ties with powerful political factions and used such connections to further expand their business empires. Sukree, for example, utilized his links with Bangkok Bank to the advantage of his thriving textile enterprise.

## The Challenges of Upgrading

Economic upgrading refers to the process by which firms move from labor-intensive, low-value- added activities to high technological, high-value-added activities. In the textile industry, upgrading might involve moving from production and assembly activities to R&D, designing, branding, and distribution. Moving from a middle-income economy to a fully industrialized, high-income economy entails wide-ranging upgrading of the country's major industries.

Despite Thailand's impressive growth record beginning in the mid-twentieth century, international comparisons indicate that in terms of economic development the country remains significantly behind a number of its East Asian neighbors, namely South Korea, Taiwan, Hong Kong, and

Singapore. The magnitude of the difference has widened over time. For instance, in 1951 Taiwan's GDP per capita was only about 30% larger than that of Thailand (i.e., $1,210 per person per year in Taiwan versus $938 per person per year in Thailand). By 1980, the disparity had grown to more than 300% (i.e., $7,366 per person per year in Taiwan versus $2,442 per person per year in Thailand). This difference in performance cannot be accounted for by the magnitude of investment – Thailand exhibited a larger average investment share of GDP than Taiwan over the period. The disparity must therefore lie in how efficiently the investments were put to work.

In Thailand, much of the investment was channeled through domestic commercial banks, which had grown to replace foreign banks that withdrew from the country during the Second World War. The banks prospered from a growing pool of domestic deposits after the government enacted policies to stop the remittance stream that Chinese immigrants were sending back to their homeland. All of the new urban industries were family based and organized around one of the big banks. Thai commercial banks played a key role in initiating new businesses ranging from agribusiness and textiles to retailing and insurance. In addition to supplying crucial capital for Sino-Thai entrepreneurs, the banks also helped coordinate industrial initiatives to lobby for government support such as reduced tariffs and favorable tax breaks for investments. In carrying out their roles as mediators between business and government, the banks became deeply intertwined in the patron-client networks that characterized the developing Thai economy.

While the bank-centered investment model enjoyed considerable success, the scheme also had its weaknesses. Specifically, the banks proved to be less than effective in compelling businesses to upgrade and absorb new technologies rapidly to guarantee international competitiveness. At the heart of the problem may be an unwillingness of the banks to allow weak firms under their patronage to fail. Doner and Ramsay (2000, p. 162) relay an interesting episode during the early 1970s when the domestic textile market faced a serious over-production crisis. Instead of allowing a major shakeout, which might have resulted in only the most efficient manufacturers surviving, the banks instead played the role of an industry mediator by trying to enact a collective capacity limit. They also lobbied for government support in lowering tariffs and awarding special tax benefits for exporters.

While the banks' mediating role helped both small and large firms to survive the domestic supply glut, the incident may have diminished incentives for manufacturers to upgrade their production technology. Specifically, why would a factory owner bother to upgrade if his production would later be held back to save less efficient firms? Thus, although the Thai government did not bail out failing businesses due to the central bank's hard budget constraint, the commercial banks occasionally stepped in to suppress market competition. This inefficient interference may have been one of the contributing factors preventing the economy's investments from reaching their full potential.

An antidote to insufficient competition and upgrading is to expose domestic industries to global market forces. To do so, policy makers must encourage exports and at the same time open up the domestic market to imports and foreign investment. These were the strategies that the Thai policy makers attempted to implement beginning in the mid-1980s and to an even greater extent in the 1990s. These policies would result in two decades of the most exciting economic adventure Thailand had ever seen.

## Glossary of Economic Terms

**Gross Domestic Product**  the total market value of all finished goods and services produced in a country over a given year. GDP is used to measure the *size* of a country's economy. GDP per capita, GDP divided by the country's population, is a basic measure of how *rich* a country is.

**Institutions**  man-made social structures such as laws, regulations and norms that regulate individual behavior and establish widely-accepted expectations regarding social interactions. Examples of institutions include family, religion, economic systems, legal systems, language, mass media, education, medicine, military, and civil society.

**Clientelism**  a relationship between *patron* and *client*. The patron provides the client with protection of property rights and other privileges such as access to resources and markets in return for compensation. Because clientelism is a long-term relationship, the patron has an interest in seeing the client succeed. The patron is thus unlikely to extract so much compensation that the client cannot survive and prosper.

**Financial Intermediation**  the facilitation of the transfer of funds from savers to borrowers. Commercial banks often perform the role of financial intermediaries by taking deposits from savers and lending them out to borrowers. Financial intermediation also takes place when a startup sells shares to the public for the first time, a process referred to as the initial public offering (IPO). The bond market also facilitates lending and borrowing by allowing governments and corporations to issue bonds to borrow funds from the public.

**Upgrading**  the process of absorbing new technology into the production process so as to be able to participate in higher value-added activities in the production value chain. For example, when firms in a country move from labor-intensive assembly jobs to skill-intensive activities such as R&D and branding, then we say the country has successfully upgraded.

## Note

1 Doner, R. F., and Ramsay, A. (2000). "Rent-Seeking and Economic Development in Thailand." In M. H. Khan and K. S. Jomo (Eds.), *Rents, Rent-Seeking and Economic Development: Theory and Evidence in Asia*. Cambridge: Cambridge University Press, pp. 145–181.

# Appendix

## More on Gross Domestic Product

As one of the most fundamental concepts in macroeconomics, GDP is widely used and has been given many adjustments for its various applications.

When GDP is tracked over many years, economists often worry that the inflation of prices over time will make GDP values seem to have increased more than they actually have. To address this concern, a distinction is made between *nominal GDP* and *real GDP*. Nominal GDP is the standard GDP measured without any adjustment for inflation. When one refers to real GDP, however, it is often in the context of comparing GDP at different points in time. Real GDP measures market value, using a fixed set of prices. The year at which prices of goods and services are fixed (for the purpose of calculating real GDP) is called the *base year*. As the prices of goods and services do not change, any changes in GDP values overtime correspond to actual changes in the quantity of goods and services an economy produces. GDP values in Figure 5.1 represent real GDP in which the effects of inflation have been removed. The base year for real GDP calculations in Figure 5.1 is year 2005. Note that for the base year, real and nominal GDP are, by definition, the same.

*Purchasing Power Parity (PPP)* adjustment is also often made when GDP numbers for different countries are compared against each other. The logic behind the PPP adjustment lies in the fact that the price of the same service in different countries can differ significantly. Prices for basic services such as haircuts or laundry services are often significantly cheaper in developing countries. This divergence can be explained by differences in minimum wage rates or labor protection laws. Countries with higher minimum wages or stricter labor protection laws will require higher costs for providing services, and therefore charge higher prices. However, the key reason behind the price differences is the fact that services cannot be easily traded across country borders. A cheap haircut in Thailand, for example, cannot be exported to the US. When the PPP adjustment is made, the prices of all goods and services are set at the same level. When the same goods and services in different countries are valued at the same price level, differences in PPP-adjusted GDP would reflect true differences in output. In this chapter, when GDP values for different countries are compared (e.g., GDP per capita of Thailand compared to that of Taiwan), PPP adjustments are always used.

Finally, it is important to remember that when using GDP per capita to gauge how prosperous a country is, the measure fails to capture the disparity in income distribution among the country's citizens. Therefore, countries with very similar GDP per capita levels (PPP-adjusted) can have large differences in, say, the percentage of citizens living in poverty. This difference occurs because some countries exhibit highly lopsided income distributions (thus causing greater poverty), while other countries exhibit much more even income distributions (thus causing less poverty). The causes, consequences, and appropriate policy toward income inequality in different countries is currently an active and highly contentious area of research in the field of economics.

# 6   Money

## Anatomy of a Financial Crisis

*Relevant period*: 1950–1997 (Post WWII – Asian Financial Crisis)
*Economic concepts*: gold standard, monetary policy, triad of incompatibilities

You can read L. Frank Baum's beloved 1900 fairytale, *The Wonderful Wizard of Oz*, as a parable about the perils of fixed exchange rates in a globalized world economy.

## The Context

The nineteenth-century international financial system operated under the rules of the Gold Standard. Every country's currency was convertible to a fixed amount of gold. For example, a British pound could be exchanged for 113 grains of gold, while a US dollar could be converted to 23.22 grains of gold.[1] This rigid convertibility rule required countries to maintain adequate gold reserves to back their currencies. The more gold a country possessed, the more currency it could print. An important upshot of the Gold Standard was that it required exchange rates between different currencies to remain fixed. For instance, by simple arithmetic, the pound/dollar exchange rate could not deviate from $113/23.22 = 4.87$ dollars per pound.

The Gold Standard and fixed exchange rates played a key role in facilitating cross-border commerce and the rise of the *First Global Economy* during the second half of the nineteenth century. For merchants, costs and profits could be calculated free of the risk of exchange rate fluctuations, thanks to the Gold Standard. Interest rates around the world moved in synchrony, because all currencies were simply different gold denominations. In short, it was an ideal environment for transnational trade. The drawback, as will soon become apparent, however, is that the system strips countries of the ability to control their own domestic money supply. When there is no new gold, no additional

DOI: 10.4324/9781003392262-6

money can be put into circulation. Such a handicap proves to be debilitating, especially during tumultuous times.

By the late nineteenth century, American farmers were suffering from sinking crop prices, a symptom of widespread deflation caused by a restriction in money supply. A world-wide shortage in gold constrained the government's ability to print money, because there was not enough gold to back it. With less money available for transactions, prices had nowhere to go but down. The United States, having given up its domestic monetary autonomy, was experiencing the debilitating side effects of the Gold Standard.

The plight of the farmers became a central issue in the 1896 US presidential election. While the Republican candidate, William McKinley, campaigned on a platform of preserving "sound money" through the Gold Standard, the Democratic Party candidate, William Jennings Bryan, championed *bimetallism*, an initiative to relax the key tenet of the Gold Standard, and allow silver to be used to back new money. The idea was that increasing money supply would generate inflation, buoy crop prices, and allow farmers to pay off their debt more easily. "You shall not crucify mankind upon a cross of gold," Bryan declared in his most famous speech.

## The Fable

It was against this backdrop that Dorothy, a teenage girl from Kansas, a state in America's agricultural heartland, is swept up by a tornado and dropped in a faraway land called Oz. What is "Oz," but the traditional unit in which precious metals were weighed. Dorothy discovers that her only hope of returning home is to follow the yellow brick road to the Emerald City, where she might seek help from the Mighty Wizard. Note yellow and green are the colors of gold and money (a dollar bill is sometimes referred to as a 'greenback').

Along the way, Dorothy is joined by a scarecrow (symbolizing the American agricultural worker), a tin man (the American factory worker) and a cowardly lion with a fearful roar (William Jennings Bryan, the oratorically gifted 1986 Democratic presidential candidate, who was a champion of the struggling farmers, but could not win in the election). The trio make their way to the Emerald City (Washington, D.C.), where they are required to wear green spectacles, literally making them see everything in green (the color of money).

Despite proving to be a fake, the Wizard was able to aid the visitors in some of their requests. For Dorothy, it turned out that the *silver* slippers she was wearing all along possessed the power to send her back home. All she needed to do was to tap them three times and make a wish. The silver slippers represented the "free silver" campaign – if there was inadequate gold to print more money, back the new currency with silver.

The economic moral of the story is simple: if a fixed exchange rate regime becomes untenable, abandon it.

## Exchange Rates and Currency Regimes

An exchange rate is the price of one currency in terms of another. For example, on July 29, 2011, the price of one US dollar in Japanese currency was 77.6 yen. If, for whatever reason, the rate of exchange became one dollar per 100 yen, then we would say that the dollar had *appreciated* (or gained) against the yen, or that the yen had *depreciated* against the dollar. A traveler using dollars to buy yen in Japan would be happy because she would get more yen for her dollar than she expected. The rate of exchange had changed in her favor. Japanese people will also suddenly find that products from the USA have become more expensive.

Exchange rate fluctuations can have significant impacts on international trade. When the domestic currency (say, the US dollar) appreciates against a foreign currency (say, the Japanese yen), the cost of domestic goods denominated in the foreign currency automatically rises. In Japan, the cost of a one-dollar, US-made, fountain pen would rise from 77.6 to 100 yen after the appreciation, making it more difficult for the American pen to sell in Japan. Following a similar logic, imports enjoy greater competitiveness after an appreciation of the domestic currency, because the cost of gadgets made in Japan would appear cheaper in US dollars. An appreciation of a country's currency is therefore usually associated with a decline of exports and a rise in imports. We would predict a depreciation to have the opposite effects.

Because exchange rate swings add uncertainty to exporting and importing activity, businesses and their supporters in the government have, in the past, expressed a preference for a stable exchange rate regime. Advocates of this regime believe the government should interfere in currency markets to ensure a stable exchange rate.

## Siam and the Gold Standard

Her economy increasingly integrated in global commerce following the signing of the Bowring Treaty in 1855, Siam officially joined the Gold Standard in 1908 with the promulgation of the Gold Standard Act. Instead of amassing a gold reserve to back the baht, the government established an exchange reserve fund in London to buttress the baht's value. By fixing the pound-to-baht exchange rate at 13 baht to a pound, Siamese currency was indirectly convertible to gold through the gold-backed British pound.

The Gold Standard was subsequently abandoned when global trade all but collapsed during the period of the two World Wars. When peace was restored, the international community again attempted to construct a new system that would guarantee exchange rate stability. Thailand became part of the new arrangement, known as *Bretton Woods*, in which various world currencies had their values pegged to the US dollar, which in turn was convertible to gold. The dollar value of the baht remained quite stable during the ensuing decades, despite frequent severe turbulence in the global financial system, including the abrupt end in 1971 to the gold convertibility of the US dollar.

## How Exchange Rates Are Held Stable

There are essentially two techniques to achieve a fixed exchange rate. First, the government *can give up free, cross-border capital mobility* by implementing capital controls. By legislating itself the power to limit the flow of currencies across its borders, the government can, for example, influence the demand for its currency. Strict limits on how much domestic currency can leave the country tends to reduce its demand,[2] therefore staving off the pressure for it to appreciate. A relaxing of such controls would have the opposite effect. Capital controls were widely implemented during the heydays of the Bretton Woods period. While the controls were mainly targeted at banks and investors, the general public would at times feel the effects of such regulations. For instance, at one point in the 1960s, Britons travelling abroad on vacation were allowed to carry a maximum of just 50 pounds in pocket money.

While capital controls can effectively stabilize exchange rates, they can also be quite disruptive to international trade and investment. For example, businesses may find it difficult to expand capacity if they face restrictions in converting their foreign sales revenue into domestic currency. Foreign investors may also think twice before committing their capital to a joint venture with a domestic partner if they expect arbitrary hurdles in recouping their money. For these reasons, strict capital control practices later fell out of favor.

An alternative method for achieving a fixed exchange rate is by *foregoing the control of domestic money supply*. This approach is similar to the Gold Standard, in which governments could not create more currency if they did not possess the requisite amount of gold to back it. Currency boards represent a modern embodiment of this approach. Committed to maintaining a fixed exchange rate between the Hong Kong dollar and the US dollar, the Hong Kong Monetary Authority stipulates that the domestic currency in circulation is fully backed by US dollar assets. An increase in money supply is not possible without a corresponding increase in US dollar assets held. Under such circumstances, Hong Kong enjoys a fixed exchange rate along with full cross-border capital mobility. Figure 6.1 summarizes the two general methods a country can adopt to maintain a fixed exchange rate.

Because fixed exchange rate regimes must contend with such serious drawbacks (restriction of capital movement *or* a loss of monetary policy

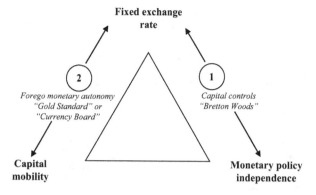

*Figure 6.1* The two paths to a fixed exchange rate

independence), most major economies of the world have gradually chosen to abandon the idea of fixing the exchange rate, and instead allow the price of their currency to 'float' according to the forces of demand and supply in the world market. This transition coincided with the ending of the global financial arrangement under *Bretton Woods* in the early 1970s. The benefits of accepting uncontrollable fluctuations associated with a floating exchange rate regime, as you may have already guessed, are the ability to simultaneously enjoy free capital movement and monetary policy independence.

Based on the discussion so far, we conclude that governments face three options for managing monetary policy, capital movements and exchange rates. Figure 6.2 depicts these options, famously known in international finance as the '*Triad of Incompatibilities*'. The term is motivated by the logic that governments can achieve only two of the three following desirable features – a fixed exchange rate, free capital mobility, and monetary policy independence. Once two features are chosen, the third must be foregone. The Gold Standard, under which most major economies operated during the era of the First Global Economy (1880–1929) is an example of fixed exchange rates with free capital mobility at the cost of monetary independence. The Bretton Woods agreement, valid between 1950 and 1971, exemplifies a system that sacrifices capital mobility for stable exchange rates and monetary sovereignty. Finally, the flexible exchange rates we most commonly observe today represent a compromise allowing for cross-border capital mobility and monetary policy independence.

It is not uncommon for countries to choose a hybrid scheme that does not strictly fall under one of the three arrangements above. For instance, a country can allow capital mobility while maintaining a 'managed float.' Under this hybrid arrangement, a country's currency is allowed to fluctuate within a limited band. If the currency were to, say, depreciate past the limit of the

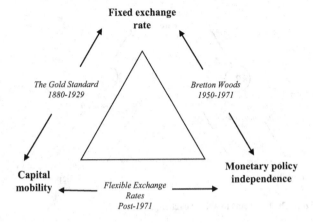

*Figure 6.2* The Triad of Incompatibilities

band, the central bank would use its foreign currency reserves to purchase the domestic currency, thus boosting demand, and preventing the currency from depreciating further. Such interventions also directly impact the supply of the domestic currency, which would in turn influence its rate of interest. It follows that fluctuations in foreign exchange markets may, from time to time, force a central bank overseeing a managed float to increase or decrease money supply, thus compromising its monetary policy autonomy.

## From Bretton Woods to Thailand's Bust: The Story of a Financial Crisis

Figure 6.3 illustrates economic growth and investment as a share of GDP in Thailand since the end of the Second World War. There is a gradual rise in both GDP and the share of investment during the two decades following the end of World War II. Beginning in 1980, the sharp uptick in GDP growth was accompanied by an investment boom, exceeding 50% of GDP at its peak. What we had yet to witness was the abrupt and severe decline in both output and investment that was observed in 1997. The aim of this chapter is to provide some basic economic rationale for the impressive economic boom and the ensuing bust.

The major change that occurred in Thailand in the 1980s and 1990s was a reorientation of the nation's economy toward exporting manufactured goods. This transformation was prompted by two exogenous shocks. First came the energy crises of the 1970s, in which the Organization of Petroleum Exporting Countries (OPEC) engineered unprecedented hikes in crude oil prices. This caused the world economy, including Thailand's, to stagnate. Then,

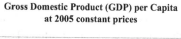

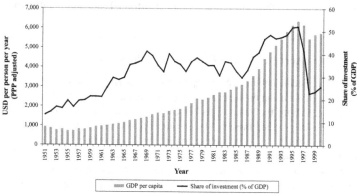

*Figure 6.3* GDP per capita and investment share, 1951–2000

beginning in the 1980s, the global price of rice, Thailand's main agricultural export, entered an extended period of decline. High energy prices, coupled with waning export revenues, put serious pressure on Thailand's public and private sector finances. Amidst this economic hardship, major developments both domestic and international emerged, sweeping the Thai economy into a decade long boom.

When US President Richard Nixon unilaterally announced the end of the gold convertibility of the US dollar (widely referred to as the "Nixon Shock"), the fixed exchange rates under Bretton Woods came to an end *de facto*. Countries were no longer obliged to maintain a fixed exchange rate between their own currency and the US dollar. Consequently, major currencies entered *floating exchange* rate regimes. Expectations that the US dollar would quickly lose its status as the world's reserve currency did not materialize, and Thailand, like many other countries, endeavored to maintain a relatively stable exchange rate with the US dollar, using the necessary capital controls.

During the energy crisis of the 1970s and the agricultural price declines of the early 1980s, the dollar/baht exchange rate remain quite stable. Hoping that exports of manufactured goods would reignite the stagnating economy, the government made a gamble to devalue the baht in the early 1980s. The country's fixed exchange rate eventually moved from roughly 20 to 25 baht per US dollar between 1980 and 1985. Note that this change was not a 'float' but a government-managed revaluation of the currency.

A currency depreciation will typically provide a boost to the country's exports. The early 1980s devaluation of the baht no doubt helped increase the competitiveness of Thai products in the world market. However, it was a subsequent change in the exchange rate policy of one of the world's largest economies that allowed economic growth in Thailand to shift into a new gear.

## The Plaza Accord and the Beginning of the Boom

After the Second World War, Japan had successfully industrialized its economy by focusing on exports. One reason behind its thriving exports was a weak yen. With the value of its currency kept low, Japanese manufacturers more easily priced their products competitively and gained bigger market shares abroad. As Japanese exports became increasingly popular, many Western governments (most notably the US) grew concerned about the ability of their own domestic industries to compete with the Japanese. In 1985, the US, together with other Western powers, in a famous agreement known as the *Plaza Accord*, successfully pressured Japan to allow the yen to appreciate significantly.

The stronger yen forced Japanese companies to seek foreign production bases. Thailand, with its cheap labor cost and politically well-connected local businesses, became a major destination for Japanese foreign direct investment (FDI). In the following decade, a number of Japanese electronic and automobile companies shifted production to Thailand. Agricultural labor was drawn in from upcountry to work in factories in and around Bangkok. The composition of the country's GDP and exports were drastically transformed – agriculture gave way to manufacturing.

In any industrializing economy, increasing labor demand eventually triggers higher wages. By the 1990s, labor costs in Thailand were no longer competitive, compared to those in other rising Asian economies such as China and Vietnam. How would the Thai economy maintain its growth if large multinationals eventually relocated to other low-wage destinations?

The large, homegrown businesses of Thailand did not play a major role in the manufacturing export boom. All of them were organized around big, commercial banks. Most focused on serving domestic markets that enjoyed some protection from foreign competition, such as telecommunications, real estate, construction, and finance. For these businesses to become the future engines of growth, they would need to significantly upgrade to achieve greater competitiveness. But how could such upgrading be encouraged most effectively?

Technocrats in charge of macroeconomic policy thought they had the answer. Beginning in the early 1990s, they radically liberalized Thailand's financial markets. Foreign banks were allowed to set up local branches. Regulation of foreign investment in the Thai stock exchange was relaxed. By opening the economy to capital mobility and more competition, the technocrats believed local firms would be forced to compete harder and upgrade rapidly. This liberalization was done while keeping the exchange rate of the baht pegged to the US dollar. According to the 'Triad of Incompatibilities,' we would therefore expect domestic monetary policy to lose most of its effectiveness.

## From Boom to Bust

Foreign investors eager to make higher returns flocked to Thailand, the new emerging star of Asia. They speculated on the stock exchange and liberally lent money to Thai banks and finance companies. As total debt, especially in the private sector, climbed, the share of investment grew to over 50% of the country's GDP. Average prices that had already been on the rise since the 1980s accelerated even further.

When it comes to investment, *quality* is as important as *quantity*. In the early 1990s, the Thai economy was awash in money. The decade-long investment boom had begun in 1985. By now, most of the 'low-hanging fruit' in investment opportunities had been exploited. Further productivity enhancing investment would require upgrading and absorbing higher technology, a significantly more daunting task. Speculation had driven stock and real estate prices to stratospheric levels, making short-term profits from betting on these assets extremely enticing. Consequently, many of the loans available since the financial market liberalization had poured into real estate and stock market speculation.

One of the most notorious cases of reckless behavior during the boom years was that of the Bangkok Bank of Commerce (BBC). After the opening of the capital market, executives of the BBC made rash financial bets and loaned large sums of money to politically connected persons who used it to make even riskier bets. Instead of punishing the perpetrators of the fraud, the central bank attempted a cover-up and used public funds to try to bail-out the ailing bank. When the scam was discovered and publicized, the Bank of Thailand lost much of the credibility it had so successfully guarded for decades.

The severity of the asset bubble grew through 1996, together with the waning credibility of Thai macroeconomic managers. Governments have two main weapons for dealing with asset price bubbles. First is *fiscal policy*. By collecting high taxes and limiting spending, the government can calm speculative euphoria in asset markets. Expecting elected politicians in a young democracy like Thailand to hold back on government spending for the sake of economic stability, however, is rather farfetched. During the mid-1990s, the government budget was in deep deficit thanks to mega project splurges.

The second tool governments use to combat asset bubbles is *monetary policy*. By hiking the interest rate, borrowing money to speculate on land or stock becomes much less profitable. Unfortunately, the Triad of

Incompatibilities dictates that monetary policy becomes impotent under a fixed exchange rate regime with liberalized financial markets (free capital movement). Interest rates on the baht were in fact already very high, according to historic averages. Yet, speculative activity was not hindered and the high inflation could not be curbed, because high interest rates encouraged even more money to come in from abroad. In less than a decade after opening its capital market, the Thai economy was heading toward some serious financial trouble.

As confidence in the future of the economy deteriorated, foreign investors began withdrawing their money from the country at increasing speeds. The central bank attempted to defend the fixed exchange rate, using foreign currency reserves to prop up demand for the baht. Negative expectations, however, had grown to be so overwhelming that the country's reserves were no longer sufficient to defend the exchange rate in the face of the fleeing foreign funds. In July 1997, the government announced the end of the fixed exchange rate and allowed the baht to float. In the following year, investors' panic drove the Thai currency to lose more than half of its value – trading at more than 50 baht per US dollar during the peak of the crisis.

When the baht crashed, the size of the foreign debt in local currency more than doubled in a very short period. Many large companies, including commercial banks, faced grave financial conditions. They had taken US-dollar denominated loans with expectations that the fixed exchange rate would continue. When the Bank of Thailand could no longer defend it, the currency's value plummeted. The burden of repaying dollar-denominated debt doubled over a very short period of time and businesses found themselves in deep financial trouble. Many were driven into bankruptcy. At the macroeconomic level, investment collapsed, and output shrank as companies scaled back their production in the face of pessimistic expectations. In 1997, the real estate bubble imploded, the stock index crashed, and more than two million people lost their jobs.

Such are the perils of pessimistic expectations in the short term. Nevertheless, it is important to remember the big picture. Even at the lowest point of the crisis, the income of the average Thai person was much higher than it had been a decade earlier. Furthermore, all losses in annual output from the crash were regained after a few years. By the early 2000s, the economy of Thailand was back on track with a healthy rate of growth. Yet Thailand's aspirations to catch up with the Tiger economies of South Korea, Taiwan, Hong Kong, and Singapore had to be put on hold. An important lesson from this major crisis is perhaps that the magic pill of financial liberalization was not going to deliver on the country's dream of achieving prosperity at the next level.

## Glossary of Economic Terms

**The Gold Standard**   The prevailing global financial system between the mid-nineteenth and early twentieth century, under which the world's major currencies maintained fixed rates of convertibility into gold. An important consequence of the convertibility rule was that exchange rates between currencies on the gold standard were automatically fixed.

**Exchange rate Appreciation/Depreciation**   When *fewer/more* units of currency A are required in exchange for a single unit of currency B, we say currency A has *appreciated/depreciated* in value against currency B.

**Currency Board**   A monetary system in which the monetary authority is required to back all units of the domestic currency with a fixed number of a foreign currency, thus maintaining a fixed exchange rate between the two currencies.

**Bretton Woods Agreement**   The international financial agreement emerging after the end of World War II, under which member countries would maintain a fixed exchange rate with the US dollar. The United States would then maintain a gold convertibility of its currency.

**Triad of Incompatibilities**   A concept in international finance stating that a country can choose only two out of the three following desirable characteristics: fixed exchange rates, the ability to control domestic money supply, and free cross-border capital movement.

**Inflation/Deflation**   An *increase/decrease* in the average price of all goods and services bought and sold in the market.

**Fiscal Policy**   The control of taxation and public spending by the government. Fiscal policy can be used as a tool for macroeconomic stabilization.

**Monetary Policy**   The central bank's control of money supply, which influences the market interest rate. Monetary policy is the main determinant of a country's inflation rate and can also be used as a tool for macroeconomic stabilization.

## Notes

1 One troy ounce equals 480 grains of gold.
2 Investors typically do not want to hold on to a currency that is trapped without a country's borders.
3 Moss, D. M. (2007). *A Concise Guide to Macroeconomics: What Managers, Executives, and Students Need to Know*. Harvard Business School Press.

# Appendix
## The Three Pillars of Macroeconomics

In his short treatise aimed at explaining macroeconomics fundamentals to Harvard MBAs, David M. Moss[3] identifies what he considers the Three Pillars of Modern Macroeconomics. The first pillar is *output* or GDP – the central variable that measures an economy's productivity and ultimately the average material wellbeing of a country's citizens. The second pillar is *money*, an economy's medium of exchange. A well-managed monetary system ensures a steady economic environment where prices are relatively stable over time.

The final and perhaps most surprising pillar Moss describes as *expectations*. People's actions today reflect their estimates and beliefs about the future. Thus, expectations can have profound impacts on both output (through production and investment decisions) and prices (through wage negotiations that directly influence production costs). The prominent role of expectations has inspired scholars to describe macroeconomic policy as expectations management, i.e., avoiding excessive pessimism or euphoria that may ultimately lead to economic instability.

Expectations are maintained by social organizations sociologist call *institutions*. Institutions are long-living (i.e., not depending on a charismatic individual for survival) and play important roles in sustaining behavioral norms in a society. Advanced societies contain numerous categories of such organizations including political institutions (e.g., political parties, interest groups), legal institutions (e.g., courts, lawyer associations), and economic institutions (e.g., central banks, regulators).

Thailand's economic success during the mid-twentieth century owed a lot to a few high-quality macroeconomic institutions – most notably the Bank of Thailand – that skillfully ensured a stable economic environment so crucial for investment and growth. The historically reliable macroeconomic managers of Thailand however failed spectacularly in the important task of expectations management after the capital market liberalization. As the asset bubble grew, they failed to take any action to temper the speculative euphoria. Even worse was their failure to regulate the banking sector.

## The Three Pillars and Stabilization Policy

One can view fiscal and monetary policy as basic tools governments use to manage expectations. *Fiscal policy*, the management of public finances through taxation and spending, can be viewed as a signal of the government's intentions and future expectations. Tax cuts and increases in public spending (*expansionary* fiscal policy), for example, signal optimism, which if done well will stimulate consumers and investors to escalate private spending and investment. This is because no one wants to miss the boat if good times are on the horizon. More consumption and investment demand tends to also put upward pressure on prices, thus increase inflation. Such moves can help restore vitality to an economy gripped by fear and pessimism. Tax increases and reduced government spending (*contractionary* fiscal policy) would have the opposite effects, and would be appropriate when an economy is overheating.

*Monetary policy*, the control of money supply in an economy, is also a tool for expectations management. By cutting the supply of money (*contractionary* monetary policy), for example, the central bank signals its belief that current levels of private spending and investment is excessive and needs to come down. Such expectations are signaled through a rising interest rate – less money means higher borrowing costs. When effective, contractionary monetary policy will calm an economic boom and bring down inflation. An increase in money supply (expansionary monetary policy) would have the opposite effect.

A subtle and often under-appreciated point about fiscal and monetary policy is that success of such maneuvers does *not* require that the government or central bank "knows best" what is good for the economy. It is quite plausible, for example, that everybody knows, say, that there is excessive spending and speculative investment that is causing the economy to overheat and driving up inflation. Yet, if everyone else is participating in the irrational optimism, it makes sense for individual investors to play along because, in the short run, everybody who participates is getting rich. It is only when somebody announces what everybody already knows – that it is time to reign in the irrational euphoria – that sensibleness can be restored. Successful macroeconomic management, may therefore depend less on insight and more on detached sobriety.

A greater appreciation for the role of expectations and stabilization policies can now give us a deeper understanding of Thailand's financial crisis. With a recent record of strong economic growth and the excitement about becoming the Fifth Tiger, it is no wonder that there was, in the early 1990s, a surplus of optimism about the future of the economy. As the stock market boomed and real estate prices climbed, it became increasingly clear that the booming economy was heading toward danger. Unfortunately, the decision by the Thai technocrats to liberalize the country's financial markets while maintaining a fixed exchange rate critically hampered the monetary authority's ability to influence investors' expectations. Strong demand for the baht and the dollar-peg meant the domestic supply of money could not be curbed. Likening the economy to a party, the chaperone (the central bank) was restrained from removing the punch bowl when the event was growing too rowdy. The aftermaths were ruining.

# Appendix
## Floating Exchange Rates

When the value of a currency is flexibly determined by market forces, its appreciation or depreciation are dictated by the forces of supply and demand. We can categorize market forces into those that affect a currency's value in the long, medium, and short runs.

In the long run, a country's *balance of trade* is the key determinant of a currency's value. Nations that produce goods and services that are in high demand from global buyers will experience current account surpluses. Because there is great foreign demand for the country's currency, the exchange rate will tend to appreciate. Oppositely, a country with a persistent trade deficit should expect to see its currency depreciate in the long run.

Domestic *inflation* governs a currency' value in the medium term. A high rate of inflation is inescapably linked to a greater money supply. As the price of a commodity falls as its supply increase, so does the value of a currency tend to depreciate under high inflation. High inflation also drives up the production costs of a country's exports, thus pushing the current account into deficit. Conversely, a country that maintains a rate of inflation below those of its peers would expect to see its currency appreciate.

Short-term movements of exchange rates are determined by capital movements. Investors regularly move their money to where they can earn the highest rates of return. A currency that offers a high *interest rate* would therefore be in high demand among international investors. Higher interest rates, all else equal, are therefore associated with exchange rate appreciations. A currency that offers a lower interest rate, on the contrary, would tend to depreciate in the short run.

# 7 Corruption

## Business and Politics in the New Millennium

*Relevant period*: post year 2000
*Economic concepts*: efficient market hypothesis, event study, book value, market-to-book ratio

In the late morning of January 28, 1986, the space shuttle Challenger carrying seven astronauts, including a school teacher who was scheduled to broadcast lessons to children from space, blew up, slightly over a minute after the launch. The disaster, broadcasted live across the United States, was especially traumatic because the shuttle launch had captured the imagination of the public, partly due to the excitement surrounding the *Teacher in Space* program.

President Ronald Reagan immediately convened a commission composed of scientific luminaries such as astronaut Neil Armstrong and Nobel laureate physicist Richard Feynman to investigate the cause of the disaster. Six months later, the commission released its report revealing that the most likely cause behind the tragedy was the failure of the O-rings used to seal the solid rocket boosters. The unusually cold weather at the Kennedy Space Center in Florida that fateful morning caused the rings to lose their ability to properly seal the rocket boosters, resulting in the fuel leaks that eventually caused the explosion.

Incredibly, economists have uncovered evidence suggesting that the stock market may have managed to correctly identify the cause of that explosion six months before the presidential commission released its findings. There were over 20 private contractors involved in the Challenger program, and the share prices of most of these companies dropped in response to the news about the disaster. Such declines were expected, because the contractors' future business prospects with NASA had just dimmed, along with the outlook for the space exploration program. There was, in particular, one contractor, Morton Thiokol, whose share prices dropped most drastically, compared to other contractors, i.e., in excess of 10%, compared to the 2%–3% share price drop for other contractors. If you guessed Morton Thiokol was the contractor in charge

DOI: 10.4324/9781003392262-7

of designing and manufacturing the O-rings used to seal the solid rocket boosters, you would be correct!

How could the stock market correctly identify and punish the contractor most responsible for the Challenger disaster, and before the presidential committee of experts had even convened? Most likely, information and speculation about the cause behind the accident was rapidly circulating in the aftermath of the explosion. Seeing the footage, insiders and technical experts probably had relatively good guesses about where the fault lay. How can such scattered insights and opinions be aggregated and released most efficiently? History suggests that it is the *market*, which reflects the best estimates of investors – people who have money on the line – that can amass and analyze such data most accurately and efficiently. Investors sold their Thiocol stock in response to their conviction that that stock price would suffer. The share price of Thiocol was indeed depressed in accordance with expectations that failure of this company's product was the main cause behind the accident (a conjecture that turned out to be correct).

This power of the market to aggregate and interpret new information is referred to as the *efficient market hypothesis*. It plainly states that all available data relevant to a company's business prospects is reflected in the company's stock price. One implication of the efficient market hypothesis is that share price movements are the best predictors of future performance (i.e., profitability). Another implication is that one should not expect to make an easy buck from buying and selling stocks because, given all the currently relevant information, share prices are neither overpriced nor underpriced.

## Event Studies – The Efficient Market Hypothesis in Action

Analyzing the share price reactions of private contractors in response to the Challenger disaster is an example of an *event study*. Researchers observe the price movement of a company's shares in the 'window' straddling a significant event and attempt to measure any abnormality relative to the movements prior to and after the event window. Events regularly studied include corporate earnings announcements, technological breakthroughs, and positive or negative turns of legal disputes in which a company is entangled. Abnormal movements of share prices inside the window represent investors' reactions – whether positive or negative – to the event, and such movement can be used to quantify the investors' expected impact of the event on the company's future profitability.

A fascinating illustration of the use of event studies is the investigation of the value of network marriages to family firms in Thailand. Since the early years of Bangkok, ethnic Chinese families have been dominant players in the growth of trade and commerce. They began by controlling the booming rice trade and later moved on to commercial banking. When industrialization began in earnest in the 1960s, these business families expanded into a variety of sectors such as textiles, agribusiness, distilleries, trading, and retailing. Despite the devastation of the 1997 Asian Financial Crisis, most major family groups survived and maintained their grip on a variety of industries. Cultivating strong business and political networks has long been a key factor behind the success of Thai-Chinese business families. A common means of growing or strengthening valuable business ties is through the marriage of the families' heirs and heiresses.

Bunkanwanicha, Fan, and Wiwattanakantang (2013)[1] hand-collected data on marriage announcements of members of Thailand's largest business families between 1991 and 2006. Matrimonial traditions among this upper echelon of Thai society were particularly suitable for the event study method because (i) these marriages were customarily announced in a widely read column in the country's top circulating newspaper (ii) engagements and weddings were typically held on the same day, so the event occurred in a single instance, and (iii) the nuptials between members of two influential business or politically powerful families has the potential to strengthen network ties and enhance the competitive advantage of the families.

Among the 131 marriages involving members of major business families during the period in question, a large majority satisfied the criteria for being "network" marriages. They were nuptials that involving two influential business or political families. Using a 60-day window (i.e., 30 days before and after the wedding announcement), the researchers estimated an unusual and noteworthy increase of between 4% and 5% in the share prices of each family's companies. By contrast, in marriages known to be for the sake of love (e.g., when the bride or groom is in show business, an academic or a foreigner), family business share prices showed no such abnormal returns.

Now that we appreciate the usefulness of stock prices in conveying valuable insights involving events as varied as space shuttle launches and wedding announcements, we turn our attention to examining what the stock market can tell us about corruption. First, however, an overview is in order of the evolution of Thailand's political landscape since the turn of the millennium.

## The Crisis, A New Constitution, and the Rise of Thaksin Shinawatra

Some scholars believe that the severity of the 1997 economic crisis in Thailand was due in large part to the nation's apparently timid and irresolute leadership. An important contributing factor to the gravity of the crisis was failure of the government to take decisive action.[2] As the financial sector continued to ail in 1996, the government seemed strikingly incapable of making necessary decisions. If they had been firm and consistent in dealing with reckless profiteers; if they have provided support for relatively healthy banks, perhaps investors could have been calmed, and the devastating capital flight might have not occurred. Why did the country's leaders become paralyzed at such a critical moment?

The political climate in Thailand was becoming increasingly democratized in the early 1990s. Fragile coalition governments took turns administering the country. Because no political party ever attained a sufficient majority to establish a stable regime, different factions constantly threatened to defect and to bring down the governing coalition. Leaders of these various blocks became what political scientist call 'veto players.' Because the survival of the coalition depended on them, they had the power to block any policy initiative they disliked. In the build up to the crisis, major veto players within the government also had significant interest in the sickest companies in the financial sector. The crucial policy actions that would necessarily have penalized these particular companies were completely blocked, thus ensuring that the woes of the financial sector would grow into a full-blown economic crisis.

Years before the crisis, a proposal had been tabled with the aim of curing the endemic instability of Thailand's coalition governments. According to the draft of a new constitution, revised election rules would favor large parties for the sake of more decisive policy making. In the aftermath of the 1997 crisis, which many believed was aggravated by policy paralysis, the need for political reform became obvious. A new constitution was soon ratified. The election in 2001, the first to take place under the new election rules, proved some of the new constitutional designs to be quite effective. However, unexpected consequences of the new laws were much more radical than anybody had ever dreamed.

The 1997 constitution was hailed as a significant triumph of democracy. Unlike previous constitutions that were written by the political elite, the new charter was drafted by a popularly elected Constitutional Drafting Assembly. The senate, whose members used to be appointed, would become fully elected. Another important feature of the new constitution was election reform. Multi-member constituencies were replaced with single-member constituencies. This winner-take-all election system hurt the chances of small parties because coming in second or third in an election, unlike in the earlier multi-member constituencies system, would not result in a seat in parliament. If big parties were able to attract popular local candidates to run under their banner, then they could quite effectively deny small parties any chance of representation. Circumstances were thus ripe for big players to engineer electoral dominance, effectively consolidate political power, and, theoretically, govern with greater confidence and stability.

The major winner under these new rules was the *Thai Rak Thai* (TRT) Party, founded and led by a telecommunications tycoon by the name of Thaksin Shinawatra. Thaksin started his career in the police force, but made his fortune by winning government concessions for pager and cell phone services, and cable television. Utilizing his already massive resources, Thaksin ran a slick media campaign, out-maneuvering his rivals who were still reeling from the recent economic crisis. With his background as a remarkably successful businessman, he presented himself as a modern leader who could guide Thailand out of its economic woes. Like all political parties, TRT attempted to please all voters from urbanites to rural farmers. Nevertheless, Thaksin's early campaign was unmistakably business-friendly.

The TRT's success in the 2001 elections was unprecedented. The party was two seats short of a parliament majority and easily absorbed a few small parties to ensure its dominance. However, Thaksin's enormous success, coupled with his brash style of leadership, earned the contempt of those previously in power, including the military, the palace, and other political parties. His opponents were nervous that the tycoon would consolidate a stronghold over political power and use it to enrich himself by bolstering his business interests at the expense of his rivals. It was in the face of this hostile atmosphere that Thaksin morphed into a populist. Sensing the deep hostility of the established elite, he introduced three major innovative programs that would forever endear him to the rural poor – universal health care, agriculture debt relief, and centrally funded low-interest loans administered at the village level.

Thaksin's populist platform represented the first instance in which the policies of an elected central government had major positive economic impact on the masses of people living in Thailand's impoverished provincial regions. Some scholars have argued that the universal healthcare program was the most successful among all previous government measures in lifting people out of poverty. Nevertheless, many other of his initiatives ended in disaster. The TRT's heavy-handed anti-narcotics policy and its mismanagement of Muslim insurgents in the south, for example, are believed to be responsible for the deaths of thousands of innocent victims. A thorough study of Thaksin's disastrous human-rights records would require a much more extensive treatment and is beyond the scope of this chapter. Our focus here is to study how public policy can be used for business interests when the power of the state falls into the hands of savvy tycoons.

Under clientelism, businesses mainly influence public policy through direct relationships with powerful political figures. However, by the turn of the millennium, 'Big Business'[3] move openly into the political arena in order to control public policy more directly by seeking office.

## The Changing Dynamics of Rent-Seeking in Thailand

Rent-seeking is an effort to enrich oneself without contributing any additional value to society. Such activities are usually achieved through manipulating laws, regulations, or political power.

In a free society, people can earn their living and even become rich by supplying goods or services that are valued by many consumers in a marketplace.

When a bureaucrat extorts bribes, for example, by threatening to close a restaurant using some obscure red tape regulation, he is enriching himself without contributing anything of value to society. Other examples of rent-seeking activity include filing frivolous lawsuits against business rivals or erecting regulatory barriers to discourage startups in an industry in order to avoid competition.

Clientelism is a popular mode of rent-seeking. In many environments, politically influential patrons shield their clients from competition in exchange for a share of the business profits, but anti-competitive behavior usually leads to higher costs and lower quality. Hence, rent-seeking activity can be detrimental to economic development. Seeking privileges through relationships with the politically powerful can succeed if the identities of those in power do not change too frequently. However, the breed of clientelism that flourished in Thailand during the 1960s exerted limited harm on economic growth because the patrons were numerous and did not control enough power to entirely thwart competition.

As the political climate in Thailand became increasingly democratized in the 1990s, it was more difficult to predict who would be in control of the government. Besides, the democratically elected political leaders would likely become more powerful under the 1997 constitution due to the new rules favoring large parties (e.g., single-member constituencies). For Big Business, this new environment suggested that the opportune moment had come to get involved more directly in the power play. They decided to gain the control they desired through elections, and other democratic processes.

## Stock Prices and Financial Ratios

In advanced economies, ownership of major productive assets (land, factories, technology etc.) are subdivided, tracked, and traded, using the concept of 'equity.' Holders of a company's equity or stock have a claim on future profits in proportion to the number of shares they own. In the U.S. and Western Europe, ownership of a corporation's stock is usually dispersed. Management of the company's day-to-day operations is overseen by a professional manager, who is answerable to a board of directors tasked to look out for the interest of the company's shareholders. In Thailand, a small number of families still exert strong control over the country's major businesses. Ownership of corporate equity is therefore more concentrated in the hands of fewer people. The management of companies also remains under closer control of the founding family members.

How can one measure the value of a large company like Microsoft? Viewing the company as a collection of productive assets, an accountant can quite straightforwardly analyze a company's balance sheet and calculate the total amount it owns (i.e., assets such as the value of land, offices, machinery...)

and how much owes (i.e., liabilities such as bank loans and unpaid bills). The balance of these two quantities (assets minus liabilities), called the 'book value', represents one definition of the total worth of the company.

An alternative method of valuing a company is based on the transaction price for ownership shares of the company. By summing up the value of the company's total stock (the number of outstanding shares multiplied by the stock price listed at the stock market), one can calculate the 'market value' of the company. As stock prices erratically move up and down every day, so does the value of a company as measured according to this definition. Although this second valuation method may initially sound haphazard and unreliable, many economists believe that it represents a superior estimate of the company's true worth. Consider a hypothetical example in which a company is hit with a lawsuit that could cost it millions of dollars. Because the outcome of the lawsuit has not yet been determined, the book value of the company remains unaffected. The market value of the company, on the other hand, would immediately adjust downward to reflect the possibility of future loss. Because the market value tends to incorporate the most up-to-date information available about future events, it is often the preferred valuation method among economist and financial researchers.

Knowing that the book value tends to be more stable while the market value is often in flux, it probably comes as no surprise that the two valuation methods usually give different estimates of a company's worth. The relative sizes of the book and market values, however, can be quite informative. As the hypothetical example of the company lawsuit above illustrates, negative information about the company's future tends to drive down the company's market value immediately while leaving the book value unchanged. News that would boost expectations of the company's future profits, on the other hand would drive up the market value while again leaving the book value relatively unaffected (at least in the short run). The ratio of these two quantities therefore provides useful insights about investors' future expectations. A company that has a large market-to-book ratio is typically believed to possess strong prospects for future profitability. A very low market-to-book ratio could signal financial difficulty on the horizon.

## Detecting the Payoff from Rent-Seeking

Among Thailand's business leaders, who were the most likely to enter politics? Boonkanwanicha and Wiwattanakantang (2008) constructed a database of Thailand's 2,000 largest companies prior to the 2001 elections.[4] Ownership of the companies was traced back to big business families. Among the top 100 families with the highest ownership ('tycoons'), 13 had a candidate running for office in the 2001 elections ('tycoon-cum-leaders'). Comparing the 13 tycoon-cum-leader families that ran for political office to the remaining 87 tycoon families that did not, the authors found some interesting differences. First, the tycoon-cum-leaders owned companies with significantly larger assets. They also had more family members sitting on their board of management.

Most interesting, however, is the finding that the companies owned by the tycoon-cum-leader families already had a significantly greater proportion of income (23% vs. 2.5%) coming from government concessions (telecommunications, media, public transportation, construction, mining, and power generation), when compared to businesses that did not enter politics. Tycoon-cum-leader families thus have their fortunes intertwined with politics. They therefore have much more to win or lose from government decisions. Once they win power, what types of actions can these tycoon-cum-leaders take that qualify as rent-seeking? Can the effect of such rent-seeking be detected empirically? We will next address these challenging questions using the tools from financial economics that were earlier reviewed.

Bunkanwanicha and Wiwattanakantang (2008) identified a number of rent-seeking policies that were implemented after the 2001 elections when Thaksin and the tycoon-cum-leader families took control of the government after the 2001 elections. The favorable new policies were directed toward companies owned by the tycoon-cum-leader families.

- Implementation of a foreign entry barrier in the telecommunication sector
- Modification of a telecommunications concession contract in favor of the incumbent
- Reduction in fees and the granting of new concessions for a terrestrial television station
- Tax exemption for a communication satellite operator owned by the Shinawatra family

By the end of 2003, one could easily detect the superior business performance of companies owned by tycoon-cum-leader families relative to several benchmarks. In terms of market share, for example, the 13 tycoon-cum-leader firms gained an additional 12.2% market share *on average*, while other companies in the top 2,000 list slightly lost ground (Table 7.1). The results are consistent with Bunkanwanicha and Wiwattanakantang's theory that big businesses that successfully obtain political office would benefit disproportionately from government policy after the 2001 elections.

More important is the fact that in modern financial markets, a business owner need not wait for future profits to materialize before cashing in. This is because stock prices immediately assimilate information about prospective profits. A company that is granted favorable treatment from the government will identify as expecting higher profits in the future, and its stock price will soar immediately. Following this logic, we should expect to see a significant jump in the market-to-book ratio of companies belonging to tycoon-cum-leader families after the rise to power of the Thaksin government.

The data in Table 7.2 bear out these expectations. While all large companies in Bunkanwanicha and Wiwattanakantang's dataset displayed significant gains in stock value during the period of 2000–2003, the gains of tycoon-cum-leader firms' particularly stand out. Prior to 2001, all large

*Table 7.1* Average market shares of firms before and after the 2001 elections

|  | Before 2001 (2000–2001 avg.) | After 2001 (2002–2003 avg.) | Difference |
|---|---|---|---|
|  | (1) | (2) | (2) – (1) |
| Tycoon-cum-leader firms (%) | 26.1 | 38.3 | +12.2 |
| Tycoon firms (%) | 30.4 | 29.8 | –0.6 |
| Other firms (%) | 28.5 | 23.9 | –4.6 |

*Source*: Bunkanwanicha and Wiwattanakantang (2008).

*Table 7.2* Market-to-book ratios of firms before and after the 2001 elections

|  | Before 2001 (2000–2001 avg.) | After 2001 (2002–2003 avg.) | Difference |
|---|---|---|---|
|  | (1) | (2) | (2) – (1) |
| Tycoon-cum-leader firms (%) | 91.8 | 314.1 | +222.3 |
| Tycoon firms (%) | 82.0 | 146.9 | +64.9 |
| Other firms (%) | 90.9 | 144.1 | +53.2 |

*Source*: Bunkanwanicha and Wiwattanakantang (2008).

companies exhibited average market-to-book ratios of around 80%–90%. After the preferential government policies, tycoon-cum-leader firms had *an average* market-to-book ratio of over 300%, more than twice as large as the average ratios for other companies in the top 2,000 large company list. These results clearly suggest that the stock market strongly believed the politically well-connected firms would enjoy significant gains in future profitability, thanks to their greatly enhanced rent-seeking capabilities.

## The Ending of One Era and the Beginning of Another

In September 2006, five years after his rise to power, Thaksin Shinawatra's government was overthrown by a military coup widely believed to be supported by Thailand's traditional elites and the disgruntled tycoons whose status and power were threatened by him. A new constitution was adopted in 2007, with features built-in to dial down the power of elected representatives. The coup was followed by five years of political turmoil during which opponents and supporters of the ousted prime minister took turns staging large-scale street protests, one of which ended in violence and close to a hundred civilian deaths. Following a general election in 2011, Yingluck Shinawatra, Thaksin's younger sister, herself a seasoned business woman, became Thailand's first female prime minister while her brother remained in exile. Yingluck's government lasted three years, before yet another coup was engineered by the anti-Thaksin coalition. This time, the military-led establishment, by specifying in the 2017 constitution that a wholly appointed senate would take part in voting for the prime minister, made sure that elected representatives attempting to consolidate political power would face insurmountable obstacles.

What do these developments imply about rent-seeking and the future of Thailand's economy? With elected politicians on the back foot, big business has successfully cozied up with the old axis of political power, the military and the entrenched bureaucratic circle. Because this new alliance is determined to remain in power and has demonstrated the capability of thwarting any checks and balances, one would expect an exacerbation of corruption and rent-seeking. Such expectations have turned out to be correct. As Thailand's corruption rankings continued to slide, the accumulated wealth of major business families skyrocketed.

While rent-seeking may be seen as a familiar aspect of business, economists believe that in excessive amounts of it can seriously damage economic growth. The detrimental effects of rent-seeking occur through the following channels. First, resources and energy devoted to gaining political favor often distract managers from their main job, i.e., running business efficiently and discovering innovative methods to cut cost and enhance quality. Second, rent-seeking often leads to a reduction in competition due to newly erected entry barriers. In the long run, this strategy inevitably leads to companies becoming complacent and losing their competitive edge. Any trend suggesting greater intensities of rent-seeking over time is thus usually considered bad news by economists.

The Thai economy has historically exhibited great resilience and has so far defied experts' gloomiest predictions. Whether this new breed of corruption and rent-seeking will significantly impair Thailand's economic future is still to be seen.

## Epilogue – Harnessing the Power of Markets for Important Predictions

In a modern economy, prices contain important information about the subjective probabilities of future events. Oil prices, for example, often indicate a perception of the level of risk of political instability in the Middle East. If investors think war is imminent, oil prices jump in response. The price of insurance for real estate in coastal areas contains valuable information about the expected severity of climate change. Rising insurance premiums signal a growing likelihood of future calamity, while steady or declining premiums indicate confidence in our ability to manage and cope with such environmental challenges.

While oil prices and insurance premiums give us indirect clues about Middle Eastern politics and climate change, other market prices are designed to supply odds of different future outcomes more directly. For example, the *Iowa Electronic Markets*, run by the business school at the University of Iowa allows people to buy and sell shares, the value of which depends on the outcome of upcoming elections. The prices of the shares for each candidate in the election indicate the probability of that candidates winning. For example, on November 7, 2016, the eve of the US presidential election, the price of a share that would pay $1 if the Democratic Party candidate, Hillary Clinton won, was trading at roughly $0.80. The price indicates that the investors believe the probability of Clinton winning was 80% (and the chances of Trump becoming president was roughly one in five). Just in case you were wondering, the Iowa Electronic Markets did in fact erroneously forecast a Clinton victory in the 2016 presidential elections. Nevertheless, in presidential elections from 1988 to 2004, the Iowa Electronic Markets have predicted results better than the polls three times out of four. Therefore, while markets do not have a perfect record, they do exhibit remarkable success in predicting highly uncertain future events.

## Glossary of Economic Terms

**Efficient market hypothesis**    the proposition that all available data relevant to a company's business prospects is reflected in the company's stock price.

**Event study**    the analysis of share price reactions to new information relevant to a company's prospects. Researchers observe the price movement of a company's shares in a 'window' straddling a significant event and attempt to measure any abnormality relative to movements prior to and after the event window.

**Book value**    the total value of a firm's assets, net of its outstanding liability. The book value is the net amount that is expected to be raised if the company's assets were liquidated.

**Market-to-book ratio**    the ratio of a company's market value (share price times the number of outstanding shares) to its book value.

**Prediction market**    a platform where people can buy and sell shares that reflect their subjective beliefs about the outcome of future events.

## Notes

1 Bunkanwanicha, P., Fan, J., and Wiwattanakantang, Y. (2013). "The Value of Marriage to Family Firms." *Journal of Financial and Quantitative Analysis*, 48(2), 611–636.
2 MacIntyre, A. (2001). "Institutions and Investors: The Politics of the Economic Crisis in Southeast Asia." *International Organization*, 55(1), 81–122.
3 For the purposes of this discussion, Big Business refers to the 20 wealthiest families that control the majority of the country's (legal) economic activity.
4 Bunkanwanicha, P., and Wiwattanakantang, Y. (2009). "Big Business Owners in Politics." *Review of Financial Studies*, 22(6), 2133–2168.

# Appendix
## From Theory to Personal Finance

After reading about the efficiency with which the stock market responds to news such as the Challenger disaster in the US or network marriages in Thailand, your initial reaction might be to leave the management of your savings in the hands of expert money managers. If successful investing requires such skill and speed, then it is better left to the professionals, right? It turns out that investment advice derived from the efficient market hypothesis is the opposite. This appendix will attempt to explain why.

According to our theory, it is the market that is efficient, *not* individuals (or teams of) investor(s). In fact, the efficient market hypothesis posits that even the smartest investors *cannot* consistently generate higher investment returns than the average rate of return for the entire market. Therefore, hiring a money manager will always get you a lower rate of return than that of the overall market, because you are always liable to paying your investment manager a fee. Luckily, small investors can secure the market rate of return simply by investing in low-fee, passive index funds. Index funds pool money from many investors and spread it across a wide range of shares so that the return on money invested mimics the market rate of return. Because index funds simply spread investments without making any analysis or judgment calls, they typically charge fees that are many folds lower than actively managed funds. The efficient market hypothesis submits that such a parsimonious investment strategy is the best investors can hope to achieve over a long period of time.

Index funds have the added virtue that, by design, they are well diversified. Events that surprise almost everybody, like the election victory of Trump in 2016, occur from time to time, and even prediction markets may get them wrong. It is therefore important not to place your eggs all in the same basket. Investing in low fee, index funds does not mean that you will never lose money – bad things happen and you get hurt some times. However, you can be relatively confident that, across a variety of different bets over a long period of time, with index funds, you will come out on top.

Our confidence in low fee, passive investment rests somewhat on the assumption that the investment playing field is generally level. If some people have a strong and unfair advantage – for example, being privileged to important news before it is released to everybody else – then the passive investment strategy may fail to produce the best returns in the long run. The unfair advantage that is most frequently raised is insider trading – company executives exploiting their insider knowledge of upcoming developments to buy or sell their company's shares *before* the news is released to the public. Insider trading is unlawful, but it cannot be entirely prevented. The degree to which insider trading can be stamped out largely depends on the skill and commitment of stock market regulators – vital economic institutions in the modern economy. Researchers have produced evidence that casts doubt on the willingness and ability of Thai regulators to earnestly tackle insider trading. It appears that company executives regularly exploit their insider information to enrich themselves through their stock market trading. If such behavior becomes too rampant, investors may lose confidence in the stock market and decide to invest their money elsewhere.

# 8 Tradeoffs

## The Benefits and Costs of Air Pollution Abatement

*Relevant period*: 1990s onward
*Economic concepts*: external cost, benefit-cost analysis, willingness-to-pay, discounting, social discounting, present value

Sulfur dioxide ($SO_2$) is a toxic gas by-product in the burning of sulfur-bearing fossil fuels, most notably coal. Exposure to the gas causes irritation to the eyes, nose, and throat, and increases the risk of respiratory tract infections. When released into the atmosphere, the gas reacts with oxygen and water to produce sulfuric acid ($H_2SO_4$), which precipitates into acid rain. In addition to being harmful to humans, acid rain destroys forests and farmland. It can kill or injure livestock, and it erodes outdoor structures.

To combat the destructive effects of acid rain, the US Clean Air Act Amendment of 1990 requires industries to obtain permits for releasing sulfur dioxide into the atmosphere. The limited number of permits issued by the government puts a cap on the annual amount of anthropogenic sulfur dioxide generated in the United States. Once issued, the permits can be bought and sold at a price determined by market supply and demand. This cap-and-trade system has been hailed as a major triumph in the battle against air pollution. The system surpassed its sulfur dioxide reduction target, accomplishing the goal in a highly cost-effective manner. Factories that adopted cleaner technologies were then free to sell their unused permits. If you were the manager of a factory that could cheaply cut emissions, it was now in your business's best interest to do so. For some factories, however, reducing emissions can be prohibitively expensive. They pay for the environmental damage they cause in the form of costly purchasing permits. Such factories then come under pressure to find more economical means to reduce emissions. Otherwise, they will lose out to their competitors.

The key advantage of cap-and-trade is informational. Factory managers possess the best information about the actual costs of implementing different

DOI: 10.4324/9781003392262-8

emission-lessening technologies. Managers are therefore in the best position to decide which technologies to adopt, when to do so, and which level of intensity will achieve maximum cost-effectiveness. It can also be advantageous for factory A to pay factory B to cut emissions on its behalf – perhaps because factory B can do so much more cheaply. If the government had mandated specific emission reduction technologies for everybody, all this valuable idiosyncratic information would go to waste. It is probably naïve to expect these managers, if asked by the government directly, to report their true cost of emission reduction. They would be more likely to convey a cost aimed at manipulating policy outcomes in their own business interests. Under cap-and-trade, by contrast, private information is efficiently utilized.

Among non-economists, it is common for the idea of cap-and-trade to stir up a sense of repugnance. Why should the government be able to sell to businesses the right to pollute our environment? Wouldn't such a system allow big business to ride roughshod over the rights of ordinary people? It is entirely in the government's power to issue, say, only one, *single* permit to emit one ton of sulfur dioxide each year. The bidding for that solitary permit would drive its price so high that businesses would stop using coal altogether. Politically, this would be an impossible move in countries with an economic and social stake in coal production. The policy would be equivalent to a ban on sulfur dioxide. Such a ban would lead to high energy prices, factory closures, and unemployment. If you tend to believe such extreme measures are not justified, at least in the short run, then the real question is how much pollution are we willing to tolerate? Economists answer this question with a benefit-cost analysis.

## Benefit-Cost Analysis: An Exercise in Accounting

The economics' quip, *"there is no such thing as a free lunch,"* underscores the maxim that every choice we make comes at a cost. In economics, *the cost of something is defined as what you must give up to get it.* If you paid $P to purchase this book, that means you gave up $P worth of other goods and services in exchange for this copy. Now suppose you sit down and spend an hour reading it. What is the cost of that? By choosing to sit down to read it, you have implicitly given up the opportunity to spend that time engaging in any other activity of your choice. Suppose that instead of reading, you could make a quick buck by walking your neighbor's dog. If you could earn $W walking your neighbor's dog for an hour, this implies that the opportunity cost of one hour of your time is $W. The total cost of purchasing and reading the book is thus $P + $W.

The fact that you have spent your money to buy this book and invested your time to read this chapter indicates that this learning experience is worth more to you than all the other possibilities you could have obtained with that money and this time. Denote your benefit (personal, academic, or professional) from reading this chapter as $B. In economics, this 'benefit' is defined as the maximum amount you would pay for the privilege to engage in this activity (your "maximum willingness-to-pay"). Your choices reveal that according to your benefit-cost calculations:

$$\$B > \$P + \$W$$

Because these resources (money and time) belong to you, and assuming that you know best what your needs are, no economist would question the correctness of these choices.

## Market Failure and External Costs

Sometimes, however, our choices inflict costs on innocent bystanders. In this case, we say that such choices entail *external costs*. For example, when I decide to take antibiotics to treat my sore throat, my choice imposes on my community the risk of accelerating the mutation of antibiotic-resistant, untreatable bacteria that might later infect my neighbor. In other words, my personal decision to use the medication, especially if I realized that I am not in dire need, potentially can cause harm to an innocent, third party. Likewise, when an owner of a durian orchard fails to chop down a tree yielding poor quality fruit, his choice, if it results in unwelcome cross-pollination of adjacent orchards, harms the quality of future generations of his neighbor's durian trees.

Individuals usually decide for themselves what to do about their health and their property, something which economists worry about from a societal standpoint. Uneasiness arises about some examples of personal choices, as when orchardists fail to cull inferior trees in their orchards or when people take antibiotics carelessly or unnecessarily. The ill effects from such poor choices end up being shared by the community. Choices whose consequences are never fully borne by the decision maker tend to bring about complacency. Antibiotic-resistant bacteria put the entire community at risk. The poorly informed patient with a sore throat can carelessly take medication improperly, being oblivious to the great danger of bacteria becoming resistant to our best antibiotics. As for the durian tree owner, the prosperity of a neighboring orchard may not inspire his good will or concern. He may eventually cut down his poorly performing tree, but perhaps only after it has already crossed-pollinated with his neighbor's durian trees, thus contributing to inferior future breeds.

To make precise the inefficiency associated with personal choices that entail external costs, let us assume that the personal benefit from taking antibiotics (faster recovery, psychic boost, etc.) for the average patient suffering from a sore throat equals $\$B^{pr}$, where the superscript is for 'private.' Assume the private cost of acquiring the antibiotics, including the price of medication, doctor visit and other expenses, equals $C^{pr}$. Given that the patient chooses to take the antibiotics, we can infer that:

$$\$B^{pr} > \$C^{pr}.$$

Unfortunately, the above calculation leaves out the external cost, that is the increased risk of antibiotic-resistant bacteria that poses a threat to society. Assume society's expected costs from this heightened risk equals $C^{ex}$, where the superscript is for 'external.' If your antibiotic use increases by 0.0001% (one in a million) the chances that a deadly new strain of antibiotic-resistant bacteria will emerge one year sooner, and such an occurrence would result in 1,000 additional deaths, then $C^{ex} = 0.0001\% \times 1,000 \times$ the dollar cost of a single death,[1] or one one-thousandth of a death. If it turns out that

$$\$B^{pr} < \$C^{pr} + \$C^{ex},$$

then we would say that, from society's standpoint, the benefits of taking antibiotics for the average sick person does *not* justify the social cost. Note that for cases of serious illness, the inequality above might flip. However, perhaps the average person on antibiotics could recover on their own without the drug.

Pollution-generating activity is another prime example of choices entailing external costs. When your car spews harmful exhaust, you probably do not feel uncomfortable or guilty about its effects on the health of pedestrians. Similarly, a factory polluting a neighborhood's air and water sources may put its profits ahead of public welfare. Nevertheless, it remains true that there are important benefits from transportation and modern industry. While we cannot completely ban all polluting activities, we can try to judiciously weigh the tradeoffs. An analysis of the benefits and costs of different choices cannot be avoided in responsible public debate. Society can seek ways to strike a balance between diverse needs.

## External Costs of the Coal-Fired Power Plant at Mae Moh

The Mae Moh power plant, located in the mountainous northern province of Lampang, is the largest thermal lignite-fired power plant in Southeast Asia. With an installed capacity of 2,625 megawatts,[2] it supplies about 18% of Thailand's total electricity demand. Owned and operated by the Electricity Generation Authority of Thailand (EGAT), the power plant commenced operation in 1978. It contains 13 operating units capable of generating electricity at a cost of about 0.5 baht per kilowatt-hour, significantly cheaper than production using natural gas (0.93 baht per kilowatt-hour), fuel oil (1.10 baht per kilowatt-hour) or diesel (2.72 baht per kilowatt-hour).

Lampang, the province in which the Mae Moh power plant is situated, is 600 kilometers north of Bangkok. Over 70% of the province's 12.5 thousand square kilometers is forest area. The average income of its 800,000 inhabitants is estimated to be about half the national average. Mining is responsible for the largest share of the province's economy (17%). However, more than half of the workforce is involved in agricultural production. About 5% of the province's population, or 40,000 persons, live in the Mae Moh district. While 40% of the households in Mae Moh are involved in the cultivation of rice, pineapple, maze, chilis, and vegetables, the district's economy continues to rely heavily on income from the power plant.

Cheap electricity generation comes at a significant environmental cost. Lignite, the lowest grade of coal, has high moisture content. It is the main fuel used at Mae Moh. The Mae Moh lignite mine also yields coal with high sulfur content. When burned, it produces sulfur dioxide, a chemical harmful to the respiratory system and a known cause of acid rain. Each year, the power plant burns 17.5 million tons of this coal. In 1992, the power plant hit the ecological carrying limit of the surrounding environment. With about half a million tons of annual sulfur dioxide emission, the maximum hourly average ambient $SO_2$ concentrations shot up to over 3,000 micrograms per cubic meter.[3] Hundreds of people living in the vicinity of the power plant experienced severe respiratory symptoms, including cough, asthmatic attacks, and wheezing. The air pollution also caused significant damage to local crops, livestock, and plantations. In addition to causing a public health emergency, the incident, extensively covered by the media, also grew into a public relations disaster for EGAT. Plans for a new power plant in Lampang were immediately aborted.

The environmental and public-health disaster at Mae Moh fits the definition of an external cost, but completely unhinged. The private benefits electricity users gained clearly exceeded the private cost of electricity generation at the Mae Moh power plant. There was an ever-growing demand for power at higher generation costs. In short, the external costs from the transaction borne by the communities near the power plant had largely been omitted from consideration. How large did these neglected external costs turn out to be, and what might be sensible courses of action to address such negligence?

A team of researchers from the Faculty of Economics at Maejo University, led by Varaporn Punyawadee, attempted to estimate the external cost of the Mae Moh power plant's toxic emissions.[4] Basing their study on the documented 1992 public health disaster, they forecast and monetized the human and environmental cost of the power plant operations from 1994 to 2024, assuming that $SO_2$ emission continued unabated. The external costs were divided into the costs to *(i)* human health, *(ii)* local agriculture, and *(iii)* forest productivity.

### Cost to Human Health

The cost to human health from the Mae Moh power plant $SO_2$ emissions were estimated in three steps. First, a dose–response function was developed for the risk of acquiring chronic respiratory diseases (the 'response') at different levels of ambient $SO_2$ concentrations (the 'dose'). Based on a 2002 study conducted by Chulalongkorn University College of Public Health, the worst $SO_2$ exposures at Mae Moh were estimated to have increased by between 1.3 and 3.7 times the odds that the local people would develop chronic coughs, phlegm, wheezing, asthma, and bronchitis compared to the control group in Lampang's Muang and Muang Pan districts, where ill effects from the power plant were not directly felt.

In the second step, the cost of the unusually high number of cases of respiratory illness was estimated by adding up the average medical plus transportation costs for different symptoms as compiled in the Mae Moh hospital database. Lost wages over the 30-year period were also figured in. Out-patient costs were estimated at between 100 and 200 baht per visit, while in-patient expenses stood between 1,000 and 2,000 baht per admission. Average transportation costs were estimated at 77 baht, while average lost wages were 110 baht per day.

In the final step, the researchers attempted to take into account the cost of pain and discomfort from the respiratory symptoms. One can think of this as the estimation of the willingness-to-pay to avoid the illness altogether. Using approximations from past studies, Punyawadee et al. (2006) placed the willingness-to-pay to avoid the adverse symptoms at twice the total costs calculated in step two.

The final estimates of the costs to human health over 30 years were ฿10.1 billion.

### Cost to Local Agriculture

Similar to the estimation of the cost to human health, Punyawadee et al. (2006) utilized a previously developed dose-response function, relating ambient $SO_2$ concentrations to reduction in crop yield. Assuming that the maximum $SO_2$ concentration measured in 1992 continued throughout the 30-year window, total reductions in crop revenue were estimated to stand at around ฿200 million.

### Cost to Forest Productivity

Using data from the Forest Industry Organization of Thailand, Punyawadee et al. (2006) compared the productivity of similar teak plantations in Chiang Mai province to those located in the vicinity of the Mae Moh power plant. The results indicate that exposure to high concentrations of $SO_2$ decreased the

*Table 8.1* External costs of $SO_2$ emission from the Mae Moh power plant (1994–2024)

|  | Human health | Agriculture | Forests | Total |
|---|---|---|---|---|
| **Cost** | ฿10,100 mil. | ฿200 mil. | ฿2,450 mil. | ฿12,750 mil |
| **Percent (%)** | 79 | 2 | 19 | 100 |

plantations' productivity by 30%–40%, compared to those not affected by the power plant's air pollution. Incorporating teak plantations in Lampang and Phrae provinces – areas affected by the heightened concentration of ambient $SO_2$ – and assuming a stumping value of roughly 3,300 baht per cubic meter, there was a 30-year cost to forest productivity of ฿2.0 billion.

Rural communities have long enjoyed non-timber benefits from forests, through the collection of fruits, vegetables, fungi, honey, and wildlife. Assuming 80% of households in the provinces of Lampang, Phrae and Phayao were adversely affected by heightened concentrations of ambient $SO_2$ through fewer opportunities to collect non-timber forest products, and that the proportion of reduction in these products was similar to that of timber (i.e., 30%–40% below normal levels due to air pollution), Punyawadee et al. (2006) estimated a ฿450 million loss from non-timber forest products over the 30-year window.

Table 8.1 summarizes the estimated 30-year external cost from the air pollution generated by the Mae Moh power plant. The total external cost stands at ฿12.75 billion, 80% of which is to human health.

What should one make of this number? Fundamentally, the estimate confirms that the true cost of generating electricity by burning coal over a 30-year period is ฿12.75 billion higher than the standard (private) cost calculations indicate. From a social standpoint, we are keeping the price of electricity *too low* by generating too much electricity using coal. As a consequence, communities around the coal-fired power plant are being excessively burdened with the external cost of air pollution. The following sections describe the actual responses to the Mae Moh disaster in 1992, followed by the benefit-cost analysis of the implemented program.

## Economic Analysis of Pollution Abatement in Mae Moh

A common-sense approach in dealing with the Mae Moh disaster, one taken by EGAT, is to follow the dictum: *you made a mess, you clean it up.*

Working with the Pollution Control Department, EGAT agreed to retrofit eight of Mae Moh's operating units with wet scrubbing type Flue Gas Desulfurization (FGD) systems. The two new units that would come into operation in 1995 would also be fitted with this system. Using limestone ($CaCO_3$) as an absorbent, wet scrubbing FGD can remove over 90% of $SO_2$ from the

**Sulfur Dioxide Generation and Emission**
**Mae Moh Power Plant, 1992 - 2004**

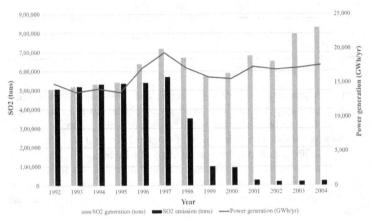

*Figure 8.1* Sulfur dioxide generated and emitted at Mae Moh

plant's emission. The chemical process yields gypsum, a mineral used in construction, and carbon dioxide ($CO_2$), a greenhouse gas, as by-products.

$$CaCO_3 + SO_2 + 1/2 O_2 + 2H_2O \rightarrow CaSO_4 \cdot 2H_2O + CO_2 \uparrow$$

Once installed, the system proved to be effective in reducing the maximum hourly average ambient $SO_2$ from over 3,000 micrograms per cubic meter to about 500 micrograms per cubic meter, well below Thai air pollution standards, but still slightly above the WHO's criterion. Figure 8.1 depicts the effectiveness of the FGD system.

How much did the abatement program cost? The annual investment required to install the scrubbers from 1994 through 1999 were 1.42, 1.35, 1.28, 2.41, 1.10, and 1.08 billion baht, respectively, totaling 8.65 billion baht. Summing the investment costs in such a way, however, is considered problematic for reasons explained in the following section.

### Present Values: A Note on Discounting

A dollar today is worth more than a dollar next year. Let us consider why such a claim might make sense. Assume you can deposit money in a savings account and earn a 5% annual interest. If you deposit your dollar in the savings account today, one year from now your balance would be $1.05. So, a dollar today is worth $1.05 a year from today. Following the same logic, a dollar next year is worth 1.00/1.05 = $0.95 today. This is because if you deposit $0.95 in your savings account today, next year your balance will be one dollar.

It is customary to state that the *present value* of $1 next year is $0.95. It follows that the present value of a dollar in *ten* and *one hundred* years equals $1.00/1.05^{10} = \$0.61$ and $1.00/1.05^{100} = \$0.008$, respectively. In other words, if you can earn an annual interest of 5%, you need to deposit slightly less than one cent today and you can then rest assured that in a hundred years your balance will have grown to one dollar! Such is the power of compounded interest.

To complicate things a little more, assume today is January 1 and you are obliged to pay one dollar on December 31 for the next 99 years. What is the present value of this obligation? To answer this question, you would add up the sequence of present values of a single dollar for each year, beginning this year up to year 99. Some cumbersome arithmetic (or a simple spreadsheet calculation) would yield:

$$\$1/1.05+\$1/1.05^2+\$1/1.05^3+\$1/1.05^4+\ldots+\$1/1.05^{100} \approx \$19.85$$

In other words, at a 5% *discount rate*, the present value of a stream of one-dollar payments each year beginning today going 99 years into the future is slightly less than $20.

Returning to the air pollution abatement in Mae Moh, we can apply the present-value tool to the FGD installation cost from years 1994 through 1999. Returning to year 1994, a reasonable discount rate to apply is about 6%.[5] The present value of the investments in FGD scrubbers from 1994 through 1999 of 1.42, 1.35, 1.28, 2.41, 1.10, and 1.08 billion baht, respectively, would equal:

$$1.42/1.06+1.35/1.06^2+1.28/1.06^3+2.41/1.05^4+1.10/1.06^5$$
$$+1.08/1.06^6 = ฿\,7.14 \text{ billion}$$

Once the installations are complete in 1999, we might assume the equipment's operational lifespan is 25 years. Over this period, inputs such as limestone, energy and water must be supplied to the system. For instance, the scrubbers require roughly 1.2 million tons of limestone annually, all of which are supplied by a quarry east of the power plant. Total input cost is estimated to be approximately 400 million baht per year. Over 25 years, we would expect the total input cost to reach approximately 10 billion baht, or 3.74 billion baht in present value (assuming a 6% discount rate). Annual operation and maintenance cost is estimated to be about 200 million baht, or 5 billion over 25 years. At a 6% discount rate, the present value of the total operation and maintenance cost is 2 billion baht.

The final cost of the air pollution abatement program is the external cost from the greenhouse gas ($CO_2$) generated as a byproduct of the wet scrubbing FGD. Carbon dioxide contributes to global warming and therefore represents an external cost that must be accounted for. Without getting into too much detail, economists have estimated that an optimal tax that would maintain a tolerable global temperature increase, while not inflicting excessive economic harm would start at a relatively low rate of US$5.90 per ton in the 1990s, and gradually increase to US$16.73 per ton in 2025. Applying these tariffs on the additional $CO_2$ generated from the FGD process over 25 years yields an environmental cost of 0.9 billion baht in present value.

Summing up the investment, input, operation and maintenance, and $CO_2$ costs over the period 1994–2024 yields a total cost of ฿13.7 billion in present value. Table 8.2 summarizes the cost calculations. According to the table, the capital investment is responsible for slightly more than half of the total cost. Input costs contribute about a quarter of the total, with operation and maintenance, and the cost of $CO_2$ accounting for the remainder.[6]

Recalling the estimated external cost of ฿12.75 billion earlier reported, the abatement cost above appears to be in the same ballpark. The problem, however, is that while the abatement costs are reported in year 1994 *present values* (i.e., discounted), the external costs (i.e., the 'benefits' of the pollution abatement program) have not yet been discounted.

What would it mean to discount the external costs? Because the cost to human health represents most of the external costs, let us consider the meaning of applying a discount rate to the human health costs. Assume the cost (medical, transportation, lost wages, and pain and suffering) to a patient with moderate respiratory illness is ฿1,000 per incidence. In 1994, the present value of the cost to a patient who succumbs to these symptoms in year 2024 (i.e., 30 years in the future) is $1,000/1.06^{30}$ = ฿174. In other words, the future harm in 30 years is appraised at roughly one-sixth of the same harm suffered today! The rationale behind such discounting is identical to that previously explained. If you deposited ฿174 in a savings account earning an interest rate of 6% today, then in 30 years, that money would have grown to ฿1,000, just enough to compensate you for your affliction.

There is an ongoing debate about the appropriate discount rate, especially when applied to social (i.e., non-private) decisions. Some economists have

*Table 8.2* Present values of the costs associated with $SO_2$ abatement at Mae Moh

|  | Capital investment | Input cost | Operation and maintenance | Cost of $CO_2$ | Total cost |
|---|---|---|---|---|---|
| **Present value** | ฿7.1 bil. | ฿3.7 bil. | ฿2.0 bil. | ฿0.9 bil. | ฿13.7 bil |
| **Percent (%)** | 52 | 27 | 14 | 7 | 100 |

Table 8.3 Present values of the external costs of $SO_2$ emissions (1994–2024)

|  | *Human health* | *Agriculture* | *Forests* | *Total* |
|---|---|---|---|---|
| **Cost** | ฿3,700 mil. | ฿80 mil. | ฿880 mil. | ฿4,660 mil |
| **Percent (%)** | 79 | 2 | 19 | 100 |

argued that the correct social discount rate is zero, because we should give at least as much importance to the wellbeing of future generations as to that of our own.[7] Regardless, let us follow the approach of Punyawadee et al. (2006) by applying a 6% discount rate to the estimates of the 30-year external costs (the benefits of the abatement program) and see what we get.

According to Table 8.3, the 1994 present value of the total external cost of $SO_2$ emission from the Mae Moh power plant over the 30-year period (1994–2024) is ฿4.66 billion. Comparing present values, Tables 8.2 and 8.3 suggest that EGAT spent ฿13.7 billion to remedy a ฿4.66 billion external cost. The abatement cost was approximately *three times* the size of the value of damages to human health, agricultural crops, and forest productivity combined.

## Making Sense of the Numbers

The standard conclusion from the analysis just presented is that the pollution abatement program at Mae Moh was *not* cost effective. The costs of the program (฿13.7 billion) were larger than the benefits (฿4.66 billion) many times over. These results hark back to the discussion about the cap-and-trade initiative, where the program was praised for reducing pollution efficiently. If $SO_2$ reduction at Mae Moh was not done efficiently, then perhaps there are ways to do it better. Consider the ฿13.7 billion present value of the cost. If we take this number and divide by 40,000, the population of Mae Moh district, you get ฿342,500. This means every man, woman and child inhabitant of Mae Moh could be given this amount in 1994 in lieu of the $SO_2$ abatement program. For a family of, say five, would they rather have the money or the cleaner air? Perhaps quite a few families would consider themselves better off by taking the money and relocating. Importantly, the choice does not have to be clean air *or* money. Maybe most inhabitants would prefer some money in exchange for a cheaper $SO_2$ removal technology, or for a more gradual reduction over time. Looking at the problem from this perspective, it becomes clear that what economists are trying to accomplish is to find out the most efficient way to allocate resources.

Punyawadee et al. (2006) were aware that their baseline conclusion – that the cost of the abatement program exceeded the benefits – would be unpalatable to many people. They present alternative estimates that could raise the benefits of the abatement program up to a level where the costs would be justified. For example, while the scientific literature linking $SO_2$ exposure to death is largely inconclusive, there is general consensus that air pollution can significantly shorten life expectancy. If early death were to triple the originally estimated cost to human health, then the cost of the abatement program would be justified. Alternatively, if the air pollution went unchecked, EGAT might be liable for damage claims in the court of law, and such damages, over the 30-year period, might exceed the abatement costs. In 1992, for example, the courts ordered EGAT to pay nine million baht in damages to approximately 1,000 people who suffered from acute respiratory illnesses as a consequence of the high ambient $SO_2$ concentrations. It is conceivable that such costs would escalate if the brunt of the air pollution was not brought under control.

Let us add a few additional reasons to justify the high abatement costs. Public trust is a crucial asset for a state-owned enterprise like EGAT. If bad publicity from the Mae Moh power plant destroyed the public's trust of the organization, then EGAT would face serious future challenges. It might confront such strong resistance from local communities that it would not be able to build any additional power plants. Viewing the abatement cost as an investment to restore some of its lost public trust could potentially make the cost of FGD scrubbers money well-spent. Alternatively, one might calculate the average cost of abatement per kilowatt-hour of electricity generated at Mae Moh over the 30-year period. Using the lower estimate of 15,000 GWh/year from Figure 8.1, a back-of-the-envelope calculation reveals that the abatement program would add between 0.05 and 0.06 baht per kilowatt-hour to the average cost of electricity generation.[8] Noting that the cost of electricity generation at Mae Moh is about 0.50 baht per kilowatt-hour, while the next cheapest option using natural gas is 0.93 baht per kilowatt-hour, an additional 0.05 baht per kilowatt-hour would seem a small price to pay if the alternative was to switch to generating more electricity using natural gas.

The discussion in this section demonstrates that a benefit-cost analysis is merely a starting point in the process of public policy decision-making. Estimates contain a large dose of subjective judgment, and therefore can vary widely under different assumptions. Regardless, the analytical tool encourages stakeholders to systematically account for the benefits and disadvantages of different alternatives. The analysis has the potential of expanding the range of options, and alerting us to possibilities of which we may not have been aware. These payoffs, some would consider, justify the time and effort of performing a benefit-cost analysis before committing to a major decision.

### Effective Altruism: The Cutting Edge of Benefit-Cost Analysis

Suppose you have US$50,000 to give to charity. Would you choose to make the life of a blind person in a rich country more comfortable, or would you rather spend it on preventing *500* people living in a poor country from going blind? Framed this way, it is hard to make an argument for choosing the former. The cost of training a dog to guide a blind person in the developed world is US$50,000. The price of the simple surgery that can save a patient living in a poor country, suffering from trachoma, and going blind is US$100.[9] The charities that champion these causes compete for donations on an equal footing.

One can quibble about the accuracy of these cost estimates, but the key message remains valid. How you choose to allocate your money can lead to massive differences in the amount of good your donation generates. Adopting an analytical attitude in the spirit of an economic benefit-cost analysis, one can derive some simple heuristics on how to generate the biggest bang for your donation buck. *First*, your donations potentially can create greater impact in the poorest parts of the world – this is simply a consequence of the diminishing marginal productivity of capital – resources have more impact where they are scarce. Nationalism aside, giving internationally is often a superior strategy. A caveat is that transparency matters, so give to foreign charities that subject themselves to external scrutiny. *Second*, money can be the most useful gift to the poor. Charities often misjudge the true needs of the people they intend to help. Giving in cash solves this informational problem and allows those you intend to help maximum flexibility. Cash transfers are also simple and transparent. *Finally*, and here is where Effective Altruism ideas become more controversial – there is no need to limit your giving to people today. Giving to future generations is just as noble, especially if you believe the correct social discount rate should be zero or very close to zero.

Ameliorating the negative impacts of global warming might be of great value to future generations. So, donating money to fight global warming is one way of helping the future world. Yet, there are other existential risks that receive far less attention than global warming, the abatement of which receives considerably less funding. Such threats include nuclear war, a major asteroid impact, or an AI takeover. Whatever the true risks of such disasters might be, assume as an illustration that a one-million-dollar donation to nuclear disarmament research (or lobbying) today can help reduce the chances of a future nuclear war by 0.0001% (one in a million). Assuming a world population of eight billion people, and that a nuclear war would wipe out all human life, then your donation today will help save 8,000 future lives (in expectation). That is $125 per life saved, which is a magnificent deal! It is quite common to balk at such calculations put forth by Effective Altruists. Yet, the logic helps us think through our choices in a more comprehensive and critical manner. If good public policy decisions should be based on clear-eyed benefit-costs consideration, then why not hold your charitable donations to the same standard? Would you forgo the warm-glow of charity gifts in exchange for giving your donations the best chances of creating maximum good?

## Glossary of Economic Terms

**Cap-and-trade**  a system of air pollution reduction specified in the 1990 US Clean Air Act Amendment, in which a limited number of permits for emitting toxic gases are issued by the government. Private businesses that emit such gases are required to purchase emission permits, which can be traded on an exchange.

**Willingness-to-pay**  in economics, the value of a good or service is the consumer's *maximum* willingness to pay for it. A person will purchase something only when her maximum willingness-to-pay exceeds the market price.

**Discounting**  the process of converting future benefits or costs into their equivalent values if realized today. The *present values* of future benefits or costs are typically assumed to be smaller than their future values.

**Effective altruism**  a twenty-first-century movement that champions the use of evidence and reason to determine the course of action that generates the maximum benefit for people (sometimes including animals), and following that course of action. Effective Altruism has been applied to career choice decisions, as well as philanthropic giving.

## Notes

1 See appendix on potential approaches to put a dollar value on avoiding a death.
2 A laptop computer might require 100 watts during intensive use (e.g., playing computer games). Because one megawatt is equal to a million watts, the Mae Moh power plant, at full capacity, would be capable of generating enough power for about 26 million (!) laptop computers simultaneously running at full throttle – a lot of gaming indeed.
3 Thailand's and the World Health Organization's (WHO) recommended limits for maximum 24-hour average ambient $SO_2$ are 780 and 350 micrograms per cubic meter, respectively.
4 Punyawadee, V., Pothisuwn, R., Winichaikule, N., and Satienperakul, K. (2006). "Cost Benefits of Flue Gas Desulfurization for Pollution Control at the Mae Moh Power Plant, Thailand." Research report no. 2006-RR4, Economy and Environmental Program for Southeast Asia (EEPSEA), Singapore.
5 The interest rate on low risk, government bonds after subtracting the rate of inflation. This discount rate is sometimes referred to in economics as the *real interest rate*.
6 Gypsum, the by-product from the process, can be sold as an input to the production of building materials. Nevertheless, the gypsum produced from the power plant is of low quality. Its market value is minimal compared to the other components in the external cost calculations, and is therefore left out for the sake of simplicity.
7 See for example, Cowen, T. (2018). *Stubborn Attachments: A Vision for a Society of Free, Prosperous, and Responsible Individuals.* Stripe Press.
8 Here, we take the undiscounted total FGD cost of ฿25.6 billion and divide by 30 years ×15,000 GWh/year to arrive at an incremental average cost of ฿0.057/KWh.
9 Caviola, L., Schubert, S., and Greene, J. D. (2021). "The Psychology of (In)Effective Altruism." *Trends in Cognitive Science*, 25(7), 596–607.
10 Norcross, A. (1997). "Comparing Harms: Headaches and Human Lives." *Philosophy and Public Affairs*, 26(2), 135–167.
11 Landsburg, S. (2009). *The Big Questions: Tackling the Problems of Philosophy with Ideas from Mathematics, Economics, and Physics.* Pocket Books.
12 Roth, A. E. (2007). "Repugnance as a Constraint on Markets." *Journal of Economic Perspectives*, 21(3), 37–58.

# Appendix

## Headaches and Human Lives

A billion people are suffering from a minor headache. They will continue to suffer for another hour unless one innocent person is killed, in which case the headaches will cease immediately. Is it okay to kill that one innocent person to cure a billion headaches?

Full-length philosophy papers have been written analyzing the morality of this bizarre question.[10] Yet, the economist Steven Landsburg produced a coherent answer using a few lines of simple reasoning.[11] First, according to studies of willingness-to-pay for auto safety devices, nobody is willing to pay a dollar to avoid a one-in-a-billion chance of death. This suggests that for most people, saving one life is worth less than a billion dollars. Second, most people (at least in the developed world) would happily pay a dollar to end a headache. The benefits of a billion heads free of aches, therefore, outweigh the loss of one innocent life, so go ahead.

The benefit-cost analysis answer to the headache dilemma may appear crude or even repugnant to some people. However, we all know that even the safest pharmaceuticals end up killing a few people every year through accidents or allergic reactions. The tradeoffs in the headache example are therefore not completely divorced from real choices that we regularly make.

Examples of other routine choices that almost certainly result in recurrent deaths of innocent people include driving, installing swimming pools, and the sales of alcoholic beverages.

# Appendix
## Repugnance as a Limit on Markets

In discussing how repugnance can limit markets, the Economics Nobel Laureate Alvin Roth, lists tradable emission entitlements as an example, alongside surrogate mother services, prediction markets, and sales of human organs.[12] While some of these markets may entail justifiable risks, completely banning them represents a significant opportunity cost. For example, tradable permits, while often framed as the selling of licenses to debauch our environment, may serve as a valuable tool in solving informational problems and reducing pollution in a cost-effective way.

An area in which repugnance-driven prohibition potentially results in the biggest loss of opportunity is organ transplanting. Every year, thousands of people die while waiting for organ donations. Studies show that monetary compensation for donors significantly increases the supply of organs that are in critical shortage. Yet, most countries outlaw monetary compensation for organ donors, a sense of repugnance being a major reason behind these bans. While there may be important moral pitfalls awaiting a full-fledged human organ market, the potential benefits from a well-designed, well-regulated market just might outweigh the costs. In the meantime, Roth and other economists have devised some ingenious workarounds that ameliorate organ shortages to some degree. By creating a 'clearinghouse' for organ donations, opportunities for exchanges of life-saving organs can be significantly expanded. For example, a kidney from a member of family A could be given to a patient from family B, one of whose members, in turn could donate a kidney to a matching recipient in family C. A donor from family C could then supply family A with a life-saving kidney. Here, families A and C could not transact directly because the donor from family A is blood type or immunologically incompatible with the patient from family C.

The moral of the story is that while markets can facilitate beneficial and efficient transactions, benefits and efficiency are not the only things that people care about. Designing systems of exchange that respect people's emotions and moral intuitions is perhaps one of the most preferred routs for economists to make positive social impact using their discipline knowledge.

# Further Resources

## 1 Durianomics

### On the Orchard Tax

Pramote, K. (2002). *Chom Suan (Admiring the Garden)*. Dokya Press.

### On External Costs

Dixit, A. (2014). *Microeconomics: A Very Short Introduction*. Oxford University Press. (Chapter 5)

### On the Problem of Antibiotic Resistant Bacteria

*An Introduction to Externalities*. (2023, February 1). [Video]. Marginal Revolution University. https://mru.org/courses/principles-economics-microeconomics/externalities-definition-pigovian-tax

## 2 Incentives

### On Tax Farming

Hong, L. (1984). *Thailand in the Nineteenth Century: Evolution of the Economy and Society*. Institute of South East Asian Studies. (Chapter 4)

### On Moral Hazard and Adverse Selection Problems

Milgrom, P., and Roberts, J. (1992). *Economics, Organization & Management*. Prentice-Hall. (Part III)

### On Sunk Cost, Marginal Cost and Marginal Benefit

Besanko, D., Dranove, D., Shanley, M., and Schaefer, S. (2010). *Economics of Strategy*. John Wiley & Sons. (Chapter 1)

### On the Principal-Agent Framework

Besanko, D., Dranove, D., Shanley, M., and Schaefer, S. (2010). *Economics of Strategy*. John Wiley & Sons. (Chapter 3)

### On Rent Seeking

Khan, M. H., and Jomo, K. S. (2000). *Rents, Rent-Seeking and Economic Development: Theory and Evidence in Asia*. Cambridge University Press. (Chapters 1 and 2)

## 3 Globalization

### On the Corvée in Siam and Its Abolition

Phongpaichit, P., and Baker, C. (1995). *Thailand: Economy and Politics*. Oxford University Press. (Chapters 1, 6 and 7)

### On the Specific Factors Model

Krugman, P., Obstfeld, M., and Melitz, M. (2018). *International Economics: Theory and Policy* (11th ed.). Pearson, USA. (Chapter 4)

### On Substitutes and Complements

Besanko, D., Dranove, D., Shanley, M., and Schaefer, S. (2010). *Economics of Strategy*. John Wiley & Sons. (Chapters 8 and 12)

### On the History of Globalization

Jones, G. (2008). "Globalization." In G. Jones and J. Zeitlin (Eds.), *The Oxford Handbook of Business History*. Oxford University Press.

### On Opportunity Cost

*What Is Opportunity Cost?* (2023, February 1). [Video]. Marginal Revolution University. https://mru.org/dictionary-economics/opportunity-cost-definition

### On Real and Nominal Quantities

*What Is the Fisher Effect?* (2023, February 1). [Video]. Marginal Revolution University. https://mru.org/dictionary-economics/fisher-effect

### On the Marginal Product of Labor

*Marginal Product of Labor*. (2023, February 1). [Video]. Marginal Revolution University. https://mru.org/dictionary-economics/marginal-product-labor

## 4 Production

### On Rice Culture and Math Test Scores

Gladwell, M. (2011). "Rice Paddies and Math Tests." In *Outliers: The Story of Success*. Back Bay Books.

### On the Rice Economy in Early Bangkok

Phongpaichit, P., and Baker, C. (1995). *Thailand: Economy and Politics*. Oxford University Press. (Chapter 1)

## On the Different Rice Cultivation Techniques

Feeney, D. (1982). *The Political Economy of Productivity: Thai Agricultural Development, 1880–1975*. University of British Columbia Press. (Chapter 4)

## On Isocost, Isoquants and the Marginal Rate of Technical Substitution

Besanko, D., and Braeutigam, R. (2008). *Microeconomics*. John Wiley & Sons. (Chapters 6 and 7)

## On the Rise of Robots

*Premature Deindustrialization*. (2023, February 1). [Video]. Marginal Revolution University. https://mru.org/courses/development-economics/premature-deindustrialization

*The Rise of Superstar Firms and the Fall of the Labor Share*. (2023, February 1). [Video]. Marginal Revolution University. https://mru.org/courses/economists-wild/rise-superstar-firms-and-fall-labor-share

# 5 Institutions

## On Sukree and Other Pioneering Thai-Chinese Entrepreneurs

Suehiro, A. (1996). *Capital Accumulation in Thailand 1855–1985*. Silkworm Books.

## On Gross Domestic Product

*What Is Gross Domestic Product (GDP)?* (2023, February 1). [Video]. Marginal Revolution University. https://mru.org/courses/principles-economics-macroeconomics/gross-domestic-product-definition-what-is-gdp

## On the Solow Growth Model

*Introduction to the Solow Model*. (2023, February 1). [Video]. Marginal Revolution University. https://mru.org/courses/principles-economics-macroeconomics/solow-model-economic-growth

## On Institutions

*The Importance of Institutions*. (2023, February 1). [Video]. Marginal Revolution University. https://mru.org/courses/principles-economics-macroeconomics/north-korea-and-south-korea-institutions

## On How a Country Becomes Rich

*The Puzzle of Growth*. (2023, February 1). [Video]. Marginal Revolution University. https://mru.org/courses/principles-economics-macroeconomics/wealth-of-nations-economic-growth

### On Clientelism in Thailand

Doner, R. F., and Ramsay, A. (2000). "Rent-Seeking and Economic Development in Thailand." In M. H. Khan and K.S. Jomo (Eds.), *Rents, Rent-Seeking and Economic Development: Theory and Evidence in Asia*. Cambridge University Press.

### On Financial Intermediation

*Saving and Borrowing*. (2023, February 1). [Video]. Marginal Revolution University. https://mru.org/courses/principles-economics-macroeconomics/savings-and-loan-definition

### On Upgrading

Doner, R. F. (2009). *The Politics of Uneven Development: Thailand's Economic Growth in Comparative Perspective*. Cambridge University Press.

# 6 Money

### On the Wizard of Oz

Rockoff, H. (1990). "The Wizard of Oz as a Monetary Allegory." *Journal of Political Economy*, 98(4), 739–760.

### On the First Global Economy and the Gold Standard

Rodrik, D. (2011). *The Globalization Paradox: Democracy and the Future of the World Economy*. W.W. Norton & Company. (Chapter 2)

### On the Political Economy of Thailand's Financial Crisis

Phongpaichit, P., and Baker, C. (1998). *Thailand's Boom and Bust*. Silkworm Books.

### On Monetary and Fiscal Policy

Mankiw, N. G. (2021). *Principles of Economics* (9th ed.). Cengage. (Chapter 34)

### On the Triad of Incompatibilities

Mishkin, F. S. (2014). *The Economics of Money, Banking, and Financial Markets* (10th ed.). Pearson. (Chapter 19)

### On the Three Pillars of Macroeconomics

Moss, D. M. (2007). *A Concise Guide to Macroeconomics: What Managers, Executives, and Students Need to Know*. Harvard Business School Press. (Chapters 1–3)

### On Exchange Rates

Moss, D. M. (2007). *A Concise Guide to Macroeconomics: What Managers, Executives, and Students Need to Know*. Harvard Business School Press. (Chapter 7)

# 7 Corruption

### On Challenger Disaster and the Efficient Market Hypothesis

*Can You Beat the Market?* (2023, February 1). [Video]. Marginal Revolution University. https://mru.org/courses/principles-economics-macroeconomics/beat-the-market-efficient-market-hypothesis

### On Marriage and Family Businesses

Mehrotra, V., Morck, R., Shim, J., and Wiwattanakantang, Y. (2011). "Must Love Kill the Family Firm? Some Exploratory Evidence." *Entrepreneurship Theory and Practice*, 35(6), 1121–1148.

### On Thaksin Shinawatra

Phongpaichit, P., and Baker, C. (2007). "Thaksin's Populism." *Journal of Contemporary Asia*, 38(1), 62–83.

### On Prediction Markets

*Prediction Markets.* (2023, February 1). [Video]. Marginal Revolution University. https://mru.org/courses/principles-economics-microeconomics/prediction-markets-election-forecasting

# 8 Tradeoffs

### On Cap and Trade

*Trading Pollution.* (2023, February 1). [Video]. Marginal Revolution University. https://mru.org/courses/principles-economics-microeconomics/clean- air-act-pollution-control

### On Effective Altruism

80,000 Hours. (2022, December 14). *Effective Altruism: An Introduction—Ten Curated Episodes from the Podcast.* https://80000hours.org/podcast/effective-altruism-an-introduction/

# Index

.

Printed in the United States
by Baker & Taylor Publisher Services

Printed in the United States
by Baker & Taylor Publisher Services